IN THE FOOTSTEPS OF
JOSEPH RATZINGER

ALESSANDRA BORGHESE

IN THE FOOTSTEPS
OF
JOSEPH
RATZINGER

THE CATHOLIC HERALD

FAMILY PUBLICATIONS • OXFORD

ISBN 978-1-871217-81-0

Cover photograph: Joseph Ratzinger as a schoolboy,
Aschau am Inn, Germany, 1932 © Corbis

Originally published in Italian under the title
Sulle tracce di Joseph Ratzinger

Translated by Sebastian Cresswell-Turner

Co-published in the United Kingdom by

Family Publications
Denis Riches House, 66 Sandford Lane
Kennington, Oxford OX1 5RP
www.familypublications.co.uk

and

The Catholic Herald
Herald House, 15 Lamb's Passage
Bunhill Row, London EC1Y 8TQ
www.catholicherald.co.uk

Printed in Latvia through
s|s|media ltd

Contents

I

IN THE FOOTSTEPS
OF BENEDICT XVI

An unexpected change of plan

To begin with I had other plans.

But over the years I have learnt to yield to the breath of the Holy Spirit. And thus, instead of writing the book I had been planning for months and on which I had already started work, I found myself beginning these pages dedicated to our beloved Holy Father Benedict XVI and to his ancient homeland, Bavaria.

This is how it happened.

After my usual summer visit to the island of Panarea, I left for Germany, where I was to spend most of the month of August.

The initial plan was to relax for a while on the shores of Lake Starnberg, one of those beautiful stretches of water that lie at the feet of the Bavarian Alps. Here, I was to be a guest in the residence of Princess Gloria von Thurn und Taxis and her family, who are old friends of mine.

I felt moved and also quite excited. After all, I was returning to a place that was particularly dear to me and whose charming lakes and forests had, a few years previously, witnessed the first steps in a quite unexpected change of direction in my life: my return to the Catholic faith.

In an attempt to describe what happened, this is what I wrote in my book *Con Occhi Nuovi* ('With Fresh Eyes'): "The decisive moment, and the one that initiated the change, arrived by chance during a weekend in mid-August in 1998." Still amazed – no less now than then – at how events had unfolded, I continued: "By chance, that is, for us who have a restricted outlook which is often closed to everything beyond our limited horizon. Indeed, we almost never appreciate the Mystery that simultaneously surrounds and surpasses us, and which while keeping us alive, calls us, guides us, and inspires us." This is the Mystery, I concluded, which Christians call Providence and which I thought I had seen clearly at work during that distant holiday in Germany at the castle of Tutzing, the lakeside residence of my friends.

I could not of course have imagined that this visit would also bring a welcome surprise. As I drew near to those dear and familiar places, I could not know that now, eight years on, at the same time in August and while a guest of the same friends, I was once again to see how Providence would contrive to involve me in another project and to take me on a journey that I certainly did not have in mind.

An interview that bore the fruit of love

It was the evening of my arrival. My hosts and I had just exchanged the most affectionate greetings, when I learned that the main television channel was about to broadcast, as a world exclusive, an interview with the Pope, who was due to visit Bavaria a few weeks later. This was one of the first journeys of Benedict XVI, and it was quite intentional that its focus was to be his native land, his memories and his own people. How could we not watch this interview, postponing dinner, and more importantly, the affectionate exchange of news that is so natural when old friends are reunited?

I was curious to see how it would turn out. Nor could I fail to think back to a conversation that I had had a few months before with my friend the writer Vittorio Messori, in which he told me what had happened in 1993, when RAI – Italy's state television – had asked him to conduct a televised interview with Pope John Paul II.

Preparations went ahead smoothly, with general enthusiasm and without any setbacks, until the eve of the interview. Everything was ready in the specially equipped studio in Castel Gandolfo, the Pope's summer residence, when the arrangements were suddenly changed. In the opinion of many people, the idea of exposing the Pope to the machinery of television was excessively modern. A Pope taking part in a filmed interview, like some film star or footballer? Nothing doing.

The preferred option was thus the famous profile that appeared in English as *Crossing the Threshold of Hope*. This highly successful volume, published throughout the world and translated into more than fifty languages, did indeed represent a remarkable innovation, being the first interview with a Pope in the history of the Church.

Thirteen years later, however, in a world changing with supersonic speed, times had moved on.

Benedict XVI was sitting on a small throne in a fine reception room in his summer residence in the Colli Romani outside Rome, and was answering the questions of four German journalists in a spirit of calm and kindness.

Despite being a remarkable spectacle, it seemed quite normal to anyone watching it on the television. The Pope was entering the houses and intimacy of the many viewers while displaying a style marked by sovereign intelligence, and also by affability of speech and manner. It was a very important event, and all the television stations in Bavaria were relaying it from the main channel. Even the seven o'clock evening Mass in the nearby village of Tutzing had been postponed.

I am always struck by the Pope's ability to communicate and to be so relaxed and at ease in front of the television cameras. His answers seem to me to be simple and direct, but also full of the most attractive nuances.

We are all familiar with the list of grievances commonly laid at the door of the Church: the marriage of priests, the ordination of women, and so on. In this interview, too, it was inevitable that there would be a question – asked in a slightly insidious tone, almost as though to put the Pope in a difficult position – about the role of women in the Church and their contribution, which, it was implied, should be more clearly visible. With his customary serenity, Benedict XVI pointed out various provisions of canon and divine law that make it juridically impossible to take certain steps regarding the ordination of women; but he immediately sought to encourage a broader vision, by expounding on the true role of women in the history of the Church, rising above numerous 'black legends'. Starting with the roles played by various key figures like St Hildegard of Bingen, St Catherine of Siena, St Brigid of Sweden and many others, he went on to emphasise the strength, energy and spiritual power of the women of today whom he admired, and who, he felt sure, would find appropriate roles.

The Pope's closing statement surprised me. He concluded by involving himself in this problem, saying simply: "We must all try to listen to God, so as not to oppose Him, whilst rejoicing that women, starting with the Mother of God and with Mary Magdalen, should have found a fitting sphere of action in the Church."

For me at any rate, these few words were full of meaning. This interview warmed my heart and made me feel welcomed, immediately on my arrival in Bavaria, by the embrace of the priest who was born and grew up there before going out into the world and becoming its universal shepherd. This was the Pope I wrote about in Rome, where I went to the major gatherings in St Peter's Square whenever I could; and I had come across him here, just after setting foot in his own land, to which he was due to return, if only for a few days.

In pointing out the Truth to a world that seems to have lost sight of it and also to have lost the hope of rediscovering it and even the desire to do so, the Pope was calm, gentle, tender, but also firm. As a priest, he was modest but strong, firm but inspiring; as a man of God, serious but also capable of intelligent humour; united with the Lord, but also welcoming and cordial.

It seemed inevitable that I should ask myself to what extent the abilities of this Pope, of this Catholic bishop who now bore such a huge responsibility, derived from his goodness of character and his personal virtues. To a large extent, clearly. But I also asked myself to what extent he was the happy product of a land such as Bavaria: Catholic from the start, firm in her faith, serious in her ways, but also warm in her feelings, fond of good music and thus of harmony, and always giving such colourful expression to life.

A pilgrimage to the places most dear and important to the Pope

It was that very evening that the desire was born in my heart to prolong my stay in Bavaria; and this grew hand in hand with the desire to visit the places that were dear to Benedict XVI and which had shaped his life.

It was an instinctive decision, brought about by profound filial devotion and by my great love for this Pope; a man of the Church who, when a cardinal in Rome occupying the difficult post of Prefect of the Congregation for the Doctrine of the Faith, had for years been frequently misunderstood and sometimes seen as a sort of Prussian general; a successor to St

Peter, called by Providence to play a role not only difficult in any case, but made still more difficult by the fact that he succeeded a Pope with the human and spiritual gifts of John Paul II. And yet serene in the simplicity of his style and the wealth of his spiritual and theological experience, he was making himself not only known, but also admired.

I wished to cast an attentive eye over the landscape of the places where he had been, to immerse myself in the climate of those towns and villages, to enter the spiritual atmosphere of the Baroque churches of this part of Germany which – I was sure – had deeply affected Joseph Ratzinger not as a future Pope, but rather as a man, as a child born, brought up and moulded in a profoundly religious land and with his roots embedded solidly in her past, before entering into increasingly close contact with the Universal Church and then becoming her supreme shepherd.

As the strange design of Providence would have it, in the days immediately before his return I was already there, among these green meadows and forests, in these towns bustling with life. I was the guest of friends who knew him well and who could help me decide on my route. Why not try?

That night, in the silence of my room, this new plan began to take shape.

Numerous thoughts raced through my mind in rapid succession. One thing above all else bound me closely to the man in whose footsteps I intended to follow: the Catholic faith which, without my having sought it out intentionally, had been freely granted to me in this very land of Bavaria. It is certainly the most precious gift that I have ever received.

But what, I wondered, was my faith based on? What were its foundations? If I had been asked straight out, what would I have replied?

Three crystal clear words came to mind: the Eucharist,

without which I can no longer live; Mary, my heavenly Mother and the supreme example of womanhood; and the Pope, who guides the Holy Church from Rome.

First of all the Eucharist: the bread and wine which, every time they are consecrated, become the flesh and blood of Jesus Christ, and which represent the synthesis of all the great Mysteries of our faith. The Redeemer, who is physically present there, brings us not only himself, but the entire Trinity of which he is part, along with the Father as loving creator, and the Holy Spirit. This is the man who, having died and then risen, showed man the way to the fullness of divine life, founding the Church in order to help us on our journey; who, in the very heart of his own Mystical Body, offers sustenance that is supernatural, simple, but also full of mystery: that is to say, the Eucharist, through which a special communion takes place between Jesus Christ and everyone who believes in him; a communion that strengthens our faith every time, as grace and salvation are given to us in abundance.

Nowadays many people question all this, starting with the historical veracity of Jesus and the Gospel. Too many people seem happy to view it as some sort of myth; but they fail to realise that, as St Paul said, our faith is not just a pious legend of uncertain origin. On the contrary, it is based on precise historical facts, on accounts which hand down to us concrete events in the life, works and words of Jesus. Everything stands or falls according to whether one accepts one central event, namely the empty sepulchre, and thus the Resurrection. This is also the lynchpin of the Eucharist, which thus becomes a credible Mystery. That is why we cannot treat these things lightly.

Then, as I was saying, there is Mary, the Mother of Jesus, the root of flesh through which we were given Emmanuel, who is God present among us. The Lord in whom we place our faith is not just a distant and inaccessible creator. The Incarnation, brought about by the power of God and with the assent of Mary, delivered Him into our midst. Because of this, she is the special path that enables each of us to find Him. How blind are those who would wish to redefine her role!

And finally, there is the Pope, the successor of St Peter, to whom is granted the God-given power to guide the Church and keep her faithful to the Gospel. The role is a difficult one, and certainly demanding, but is vital for the unity of the faith and for its orthodoxy. As the Latin term *pontifex* suggests, the Pope is called to act as a bridge between God's people and Heaven, and to link the natural and the supernatural in a synthesis that is both alive and life-giving. Having been granted the spiritual powers to guide us at all times, and most especially in these difficult ones, the Pope is a man who deserves to be loved and listened to.

The next morning I woke up full of enthusiasm for this new adventure that had won me over and that I had decided to undertake.

Naturally, I discussed it immediately with my friend Gloria von Thurn und Taxis. Having listened carefully, she said, with the charming and contagious warmth that is her hallmark, that she was amazed that we had not thought of it before. I asked her whether she would be prepared to accompany me. She immediately agreed, adding that she would also be my driver and guide!

Anyone who has read my books knows that I have been a friend of Gloria's for many years. Her faith was the starting point for my own conversion. She is strong, single-minded and serious, but also capable of fun and laughter. Widowed early and left with three small children, she not only took charge of a troubled House, but as a mother with deep faith and healthy Catholic principles, was able to see her family through difficult times with the help of prayer.

I was aware that she had known Benedict XVI well since he had been a cardinal, but I had never asked her how she had met him. Now seemed the right time to find out.

She told me that she had first met Joseph Ratzinger in 1985, when, after John Paul II had called him to Rome as Prefect of the Congregation for the Doctrine of the Faith, he returned to Regensburg as papal delegate for the feast of St Wolfgang, the town's patron saint. In this capacity, he celebrated Mass in the church of St Emmeram, part of the same huge complex that also embraces the palace of the Thurn and Taxis family.

"What struck me," said Gloria, "was that he did not read out an address that he had prepared in advance. He was direct, persuasive, and a good communicator. I was deeply impressed and moved. It was as though I were listening to a saint. From that day on," she continued, "he was my favourite cardinal. I tried to meet him whenever he came to Munich or Regensburg. That's how I also met his secretary, Monsignor Josef Clemens, who is now a bishop and Secretary of the Pontifical Council for the Laity. Once, Clemens accompanied myself and various members of my family to Jerusalem during Holy Week, to retrace the footsteps of Jesus."

"As a result of that journey to the Holy Land, we became friends, and I was able to meet the Cardinal fairly often. During another of Ratzinger's visits to Regensburg, Monsignor Bertone, now the Secretary of State at the Vatican, was a guest in the Cardinal's house, and I invited them both to lunch at the palace. I asked His Eminence if he would be willing to celebrate Mass in the private chapel there, and he agreed, with simple pleasure. So he celebrated the Eucharist and then showed great interest when shown around the main reception rooms, which are now a museum."

It was now even clearer why Gloria had immediately welcomed the idea of a journey following in the footsteps of Benedict XVI and had fully shared my enthusiasm.

However, we decided that it was only after 15 August that we would set out on this inspiring tour, which, the more we discussed it and the more it occupied our thoughts and hearts, began to take on the character of a pilgrimage. But we did not want to miss a Mass which was to take place on that day, in Regensburg cathedral, which was to be celebrated by the bishop and in which Gloria was involved. Indeed, it was her efforts that had brought about the revival of the Marian Congregation for Women (photo 38), a group that specially revered the Madonna, attributing the strength of their own Christian faith to the protection and intercession of Mary, the Mother of Jesus. This initiative had aroused great interest, so much so that it had already attracted a membership of two hundred women.

I was immediately invited to attend as well, and accepted with joy. It was a way to further strengthen my spiritual bonds with Regensburg. I also thought that there could be no better way of starting out on the journey that lay ahead of us, than to place ourselves under the mantle of Mary on the very day that the Church celebrates her Assumption into Heaven.

II

A LAND LINKED
TO ROME BY FAITH

The elements of unity

Being a true Bavarian, Joseph Ratzinger is deeply attached to his native land in south-east Germany, between the Alps and the cold plains of the north.

Like the southern part of any nation, Bavaria has a warmth and an atmosphere of special joy that all visitors feel in the air. This must be one of the reasons why we Italians from the south of Europe feel at home there. If there is anything that we might find difficult, it is a certain rigidity in the German way of thinking, which can be at odds with our more flexible and approximate approach. In other words, whilst for them 'no' means 'no', for us it often means 'perhaps'; and whilst the Germans are careful planners, the Italians have the gift of being able to improvise imaginatively.

Thus, Joseph Ratzinger is often told that Munich is Italy; a rather extravagant affirmation with which I do not think he agrees entirely. Nevertheless, he is fond of emphasising the links between the two peoples: "Bavaria and Rome are certainly not that far apart geographically, and have enjoyed a fruitful relationship over the centuries," he once said to a group of his fellow-countrymen. "The Gospel was brought here from Rome, and Bavaria was strongly Catholic, especially in the sixteenth and seventeenth centuries. The still visible evidence of this is the Bavarian Baroque style, which bears witness to the great piety of this people." He went on to point out that in more recent times, his native land has given the Church a number of figures of exemplary gentleness and humanity, like Brother Conrad, the humble and much-loved friar who was canonised having served as the porter at the Marian shrine of Altötting. "In this good and humble man," he added, "we see the incarnation of all that is best in our people when faith leads them to the realisation of their fullest potential."

Still reflecting on how many saints are simple people, like, for example, Bernadette Soubirous, the visionary from Lourdes, the Pope added that far from representing a loss of the Church's cultural and historical influence, this demonstrated the truth of the passage in the Gospel according to St Matthew, in which Jesus points out that those who are granted the power to perceive the Mystery are often not the learned and intelligent, but the young and humble. In a world which seems to measure human achievement solely in terms of visible and worldly success, this is an important message.

A short history of Germany's Catholic enclave

The ancient land of Bavaria is often referred to as Germany's Catholic enclave, since out of about thirteen million inhabitants, more than half are practising Catholics. This makes it quite different from the rest of Germany, which in the north is mainly Protestant. Being descended from the Borghese Pope Paul V, one of the leading figures of the Counter Reformation, I cannot fail to mention Martin Luther. Let us not forget that the road from Munich to Berlin goes through Wittenberg, where the Reformation began when Luther nailed his famous theses to the church door of the castle; and there is no doubt that one of the causes of the Reformation was the mistrust that these northern people felt towards Rome and her Latin ways.

Let us now attempt – briefly and by no means exhaustively – to retrace the history of Bavaria.

The first settlements known to history were Celtic, and then Roman. The remains of Roman roads are still visible in many places, witness to an ancient past with deep roots, and one of which the Bavarians are very proud. The sons of the great empire in the south had enjoyed numerous military victories thanks to which they had expanded with ease into every part of Europe, and would certainly have advanced well beyond Bavaria; except that strong and determined resistance from the German tribes – including the Cimbri – forced them to halt. Their expansionist policy then became defensive, with the creation of a new province called Rhaetia, whose northern boundary was formed by the Danube, and with the building, under the Roman emperor Vespasian, of the *limes*, a fortified line that the emperor's successors turned into a veritable barrier 340 miles long.

Well before Constantine embraced the Christian God, the soldiers of the Roman garrisons carried their culture and civilisation beyond the Alps, and with it the Christian faith, although for several centuries it made little progress against the fury of the barbarian invasions.

Then around the seventh century a handful of brave and saintly monks from Gaul, Ireland and England brought the Gospel back to this land, and before long Christianity had established firm roots in the area between Regensburg, Passau and Freising. Here, the followers of St Benedict built magnificent monasteries, and Salzburg – although now part of Austria, it shares a common culture with Bavaria – became the town which shaped the area's history and culture until the Napoleonic era.

For about seven hundred years the Wittelsbach family maintained the unity of the Bavarian people in terms of politics, culture, religion and traditions. The present head of this most ancient house is Duke Franz of Bavaria, a kind and reserved gentleman who lives in a fabulous apartment, itself almost a gallery of modern art, in the famous palace of Nymphenburg in Munich which was once the summer residence of this great ruling family.

It was only in 1918 that the country became the State of Bavaria; but after Hitler came to power, political freedom was lost. Munich became the capital of the National Socialist Party, and Nuremberg the setting for its huge rallies. I should make it clear that although Hitler's rise started in Bavaria and although his base remained there, he did not obtain power with Catholic votes.

After the defeat of Germany at the end of the Second World War, the Americans occupied Bavaria and oversaw its public and social life. In the parliamentary elections that took place one year after the end of the conflict, the CSU (Christian Social Union) won, remaining in power, with rare intervals, to this very day.

Almost all the Bavarians I know are keen to point out that during the 1950s the country was transformed, becoming a modern and technologically advanced state. The World Cup, which Germany hosted in 2006, also gave the country the opportunity to display its prosperity. Bavaria has nevertheless enjoyed a controlled and sensible form of development which has ensured the partial conservation of its rural identity and has limited industrialisation to specific areas, thus preserving the country as a whole. So when you travel around Bavaria, you can still enjoy the beauty of the meadows and forests, of the well-tended fields, and of the fabulous castles that give this land its romantic feel; whilst at the same time you cannot fail to admire the towns which, in spite of having undergone rapid development, have kept their human dimension, thanks to the careful conservation and planning of the old centres and the many parks in the middle of the urban areas.

While visiting these places I soon realised that the people here see themselves as more Bavarian than German, and that this proud identity is based on three fundamental things: tradition, family, and faith. I think it is precisely this triad of values that has allowed the country to suffer only limited damage from the effects of full-speed secularisation. The deep roots of an ancient Christian tradition and a profound Marian piety have, I believe, preserved faith itself; a faith which, if it sometimes seemed to be buried under the ashes, has now re-emerged after the storms that have shaken the Church over the last decades.

Their strong attachment to their cultural roots also determines the happiness and openness with which these people express their Catholicism. Talking about the way in which faith is experienced in his own land, the Pope himself described it as joyful and colourful, just like the area's particular style of Baroque, which although overburdened, is nevertheless harmonious, and is to be found not only in churches built at the time, but also in the remodelling of numerous pre-Baroque churches. An abundance not just of decoration, but also of statues of saints and fine altarpieces embellishes these sacred places, almost as though they were colourful gardens; places in which you feel you are returning to your family, with the Father, the Son and the Holy Ghost, and also Mary, the mother full of goodness, and numerous brothers – the saints who set out before us on the path of the Gospel and who now watch over us affectionately from Heaven, generously offering friendship and protection.

The Bavarian spirit is incarnated as an enrichment of every aspect of life: from the rich and varied music that accompanies the liturgy and celebrates its Mysteries, to a love of conviviality. This latter finds expression in rich and succulent foods washed down among friends with generous quantities of beer; indoors, or – as soon as the weather permits – in the many *Biergarten*, the large beer gardens outside the *Gasthöfe* (guesthouses) in the middle of which large chestnut trees create a green mantle offering protection from the sun.

Bavaria is one of the biggest producers of beer in the world. Every small town has its brewery, although over recent decades numerous smaller ones have been bought up by the larger producers. Beer has been drunk everywhere since ancient Egyptian times, although we Romans always preferred wine, considering it a more refined beverage. The real improvement in the quality of beer occurred in the Middle Ages, thanks to innovative processes introduced in monasteries, with hops being used for the first time. Although I prefer to see it spilling out from large jugs rather than consume it myself, this drink has always been enjoyed at all levels of society, and is also often used for medicinal purposes. It is said that Pope Gregory the Great gave to the poor a gift of beer that he had received from Theodolinda, the Queen of Lombardy. It was only at the beginning of the nineteenth century that most of the breweries passed into lay hands, although the beers themselves often kept the old names based on the various religious Orders. The number of different beers is huge, and the choice immense: non-alcoholic varieties, bitters and lagers; beers made with fruit or malt; aromatic varieties or ones made with hops. It is enough to confuse anyone who is not an expert.

Not only does the Bavarian variety of Catholicism relish life, but it also fully enjoys all those agreeable things which, with God's help, the imagination of man is capable of producing.

In some ways it also acts as a counterbalance to the severity of Lutheranism, which saw churches stripped and reduced to the bare essentials, and the liturgy deprived of much of its appeal and mystery.

A special way of celebrating feast days

After everything that we have seen so far, it seems understandable that the Bavarians have their own way of celebrating feast days. Even today the most important liturgical dates still feature on the calendar. Thus one's own saint's day, the feast day of the saint after whom one is named, is celebrated here far more than in Italy, and has the same status as a birthday, with cake and presents all part of it.

Among the numerous Bavarian traditions there is one of which I have become particularly fond over the years: the celebration of Advent, when every house prominently displays a crown made out of pine needles held together with an invisible wire, and with four candles set in it. Every Sunday before Christmas one of these candles is lit, so as to mark the approach of the great day on which the Son of God was born.

On the other hand, the 6 December is the feast of St Nicholas, the nobly-born bishop of Myra. Even as a child, he displayed remarkable gifts of charity and piety. Imprisoned under Diocletian, he remained incarcerated until the era of Constantine. For centuries, and right up to the present day, the cathedral in Bari that bears his name has been a centre of pilgrimage, partly because the strange substance – 'manna' – that emanates from his tomb is distributed among the pilgrims and is considered a panacea for physical and moral ills.

In Germany every child eagerly awaits the feast of St Nicholas, since it is he who is supposed to bring Christmas presents. By tradition, no-one is allowed into the room where the crib and the Christmas tree are displayed until the Angelus has rung on the evening of 24 December. Then the whole family kneels down in front of the crib, where Jesus is lying in the manger, and the Gospel according to St Luke is read out. Only at the end of this ritual are greetings exchanged and presents opened.

Now they have a Pope as well!

How much wealth, therefore, there is in Bavaria, waiting for us to discover it with the help of the Pope, who is in every way a son of this land! When, in the past, I thought of this region, what immediately came to mind was its natural beauty, as well as the flowing harmonies of the music of Wagner and Mozart; and on a rather less elevated level, but an important one nonetheless, the endless different types of pastry in the tempting *Bäckerien* which are more like boutiques than bakeries, or the mountains of steaming *Würstel* that you find everywhere and at all times of the day, or jugs overflowing with beer.

Now, however, the first association that comes to mind is inevitably Pope Benedict XVI, a Bavarian *par excellence* and – for me as a Catholic – the expression of all that is best about this country. I smile as I write this, since I have often noticed how in some ways the Bavarians resemble us Romans in having an attitude that is a bit complacent. Like us, they have everything: nature and culture, art and music, as well as a carefree disposition and all the small pleasures that make life more agreeable. And now – incredible but true – they have their Pope as well! Is this too much luck?

As we have seen, the Bavarian character is perhaps best defined by their pride in their own traditions. Even the Constitution refers to this country as 'the Free State of Bavaria', and unlike in other German states, this freedom is based on the preservation of their own cultural heritage.

One of the ways in which their attachment to their roots is expressed is a love of folk music and a fondness for dressing up in traditional costumes. The *Trachten* and the *Lederhosen* have always been worn by peasants on feast days, and reflect the agricultural origins of society. Under the Empress Maria Teresa of Austria a fully-fledged 'peasant fashion' came into being, and even today it has not been reduced to the level of mere folklore, but is almost always linked to a particular parish or area, with local variations in the costumes and accessories. The men wear a plain white shirt, or a checked one, and a decorated jacket called a *Janker*. Their leather trousers are embroidered with red or green floral motifs. Their hats have suede rosettes and often have badges pinned to them. In some areas they wear a cone-shaped hat with tassels on it: red if they are unmarried, green if they are married. They also wear a leather belt or braces embroidered with motifs that vary from region to region.

The women's costumes are colourful and varied. The bodices are decorated with flower motifs, often embroidered by hand. The long skirts are covered by silk aprons that vary according to the season and the circumstances. The shirts have lace collars and cuffs.

These costumes have another important function: since they are more or less the same for everyone, they bring people together by eliminating all social differences and by emphasising the communal element and the sense of belonging to a region and a homeland. The result is that everyone feels first and foremost a Bavarian.

As I have often said, the election of Benedict XVI gave me the joyous surprise of seeing a friend and cardinal become Pope. This is hardly a common occurrence, nor one that is likely to happen more than once in a lifetime.

Even before his rise to fame, I never made a secret of my devotion to Joseph Ratzinger both as a man and as a thinker. From the moment when I first had the honour of meeting him, I have never missed any opportunity to report on his activities, or listen to him talk, or just say hello; because although reserved, Joseph Ratzinger has always been most friendly towards those who approach him, myself included.

Even though he has never sought fame or exposure, and even though he is perhaps a bit shy, his sincerity and the manifest goodness of his words and actions have meant that wherever he has gone, he has always had faithful friends; and this most especially in his homeland. He thus has a small company of people who are ready to help him whenever they can, to carry out his wishes, and through him to serve that same Jesus whose most thoughtful follower and witness he has always been.

When, therefore, I decided that I would visit the places that are dear to him and that had witnessed his birth and then seen him grow up to become first a priest and theologian, and then bishop and cardinal, I realised the importance of seeing not only the places concerned, but perhaps even more than that, of meeting and getting to know the people who had always been close to him; people who could tell me of words and actions that were perhaps still unknown to others, but which had left their mark on the hearts and minds of his friends.

Needless to say, Gloria was invaluable in helping to arrange this part of such an personal journey, and was a formidable *passe-partout* who opened many doors which would otherwise have remained closed to me.

III

IN MUNICH AND FREISING:
THEOLOGIAN AND PASTOR

We start in the capital

When Gloria and I were deciding on the best place to start our journey, we opted for what might at first seem a rather strange choice: namely, to keep for later the places where Ratzinger spent his childhood and adolescence – the region bordered by the rivers Inn and Salzach – and to start instead from Munich, the capital of Bavaria as well as the city which was a vital influence in the life of the future Pope. Indeed, it was here that he studied theology before going on to teach it as a young and increasingly well-known theologian whose early work and opinions were by no means uncontroversial; and Munich was also the city in which he was ordained as a priest, where he first worked as a pastor, and to which he returned as a bishop and as a cardinal.

It seemed to us that the places and events that formed the background of his adult life as a student and pastor might throw light on the years of his childhood and adolescence, enabling us to sense the things from that period that were formative for the future priest, theologian and bishop who was to leave Bavaria and reach the very apex of the Church.

A city with a Mediterranean feel

This was not my first visit to Munich: I had also come here frequently before I knew the von Thurn und Taxis family. At that time my hosts were Willy and Sonia Bogner, to whom I remain grateful for having introduced me, among other things, to the *Oktoberfest*, the famous beer festival that takes place every autumn.

As Gloria and I were driving here from Regensburg, I could hardly fail to relive the feelings that I had experienced so often when flying in to the city.

Coming here from Italy, and especially from Rome, you almost never know what you are going to find. The weather in the two places is often entirely different. You might leave with the sun shining, only to arrive here in thick grey clouds.

But if the Föhn – the warm south wind – is blowing, a magical spectacle awaits you. The sky then turns a special shade of blue that forms a marvellous contrast to the deep green of the meadows that are scattered throughout this happy land.

In the winter, on the other hand, everything is covered by the white mantle of the snow that falls abundantly over the Bavarian Alps, as it does on the rest of the region, creating an atmosphere of silence and mystery. Seen from an aeroplane, the mountains, so clear and bright, are one of nature's most remarkable spectacles. You realise that every peak has its own well-defined character, that every summit is unique. It is almost as though some invisible hand had placed them here and there, leaving footholds for just a few villages to cling to the sides of the dark valleys. From the window of an aeroplane, these are surreal places where time seems to have stopped.

On landing, you immediately realise that you are in Bavaria, since the suitcases appear on the carousel before you even reach the luggage reclaim area. And another thing that you find nowhere else: as soon as you leave the airport, you are welcomed by a strange smell – the clean, fresh air carries the unmistakable odour of cow dung, which hangs over everything and is happily accepted by the locals, since there is no better fertiliser for the fields.

Immediately afterwards, the first Bavarian you meet will welcome you with the traditional local greeting: *Grüß Gott* ("May God greet you"), which although nowadays lacking any deep meaning, is nevertheless a sign of the faith that has lasted for centuries and that still pervades this region.

Munich is an attractive and welcoming city with a Mediterranean feel to it. According to some sources, it was founded in the eighth century, when the monastery of Tegernsee was home to a community of Benedictine monks. Thus the name *zu den Mönchen*, or 'where the monks are'.

Its foundation is more traditionally attributed to Henry the Lion, the Guelph prince who back in 1158 built a bridge over the river Isar in order to control the salt route which passed through this place – salt being then seen as a sort of white gold. Many other towns, which we will come across in the pages that follow, grew and developed as a result of this trade.

Let us now start our visit of the city. Its real heart is Marienplatz (photo 2) with its ancient palaces, the famous tower of the Neues Rathaus (New Town Hall) whose musical clock plays different tunes according to the time of day, and the Mariensäule. This column bearing a statue of the Madonna was erected in 1638 by Maximilian I in honour of the patron saint of Bavaria, and symbolises the attachment of the people of Bavaria to the cult of Mary.

I have already mentioned the period when Ratzinger was an archbishop and then a cardinal in Munich and in nearby Freising – five years, starting in 1977, which were not easy. Indeed, it is well known that in this region the faith of numerous people lives side by side with a certain anti-clerical attitude, and that the winds of a liberal mentality have made themselves felt.

The archbishop's church or cathedral is the Frauenkirche (photo 1), whose onion-domed twin towers are a symbol of the city. It is remarkable that these towers escaped destruction during the air-raids of the Second World War. This majestic church has a sparse and austere interior in which the whiteness of the walls and columns is nevertheless welcoming and reflects the spiritual values of our modern era.

Looking round this cathedral, I recalled the passage in Joseph Ratzinger's autobiography in which he describes how he was consecrated a bishop within these walls: "It was a splendid day in the early summer, on the eve of Pentecost. The cathedral, which gave an impression of sobriety following its reconstruction at the end of the Second World War, was decked out magnificently, creating a mood of joy that was irresistibly welcoming." He immediately went on to point out that the consecration that took place here was extremely important for him, since "what was started on that day with the laying-on of hands in the cathedral of Munich is still the very basis of my life."

When he wrote these words, Ratzinger was Prefect of the Congregation for the Doctrine of the Faith. He then became Pope; but I think that these words are as true today as they were then. Let us not forget that the Pope is, first and foremost, the Bishop of Rome.

Nearby, in the oldest parish in the city, is the church of St Peter with its 92-metre high bell tower. Referred to by the locals as 'Alter Peter' or 'Old Peter', this splendid Baroque church is a great favourite of Joseph Ratzinger's. Its ceiling is entirely covered in frescos, whilst life-size wooden statues of the Apostles line the nave. Above the altar stands a large statue of St Peter wearing a precious tiara. Tradition dictates that it is taken off whenever a Pope dies, only to be put back – this rite being marked with a solemn procession – when a new one is elected.

St Peter's is the right place for those who like traditional liturgy, who are seeking a dignified setting, and who wish to receive communion kneeling down. The altar is still placed as it was before the liturgical reforms introduced by the Council, in other words facing the east, where the Light – Christ – first appears. But the new parish priest has apparently announced that he wants to have it facing the congregation, as now happens in almost every church. Who knows whether the reform of the reform, which Ratzinger is known to favour, will succeed in preventing this!

Whether the altar faces one direction or another might seem a small detail, but it is not. When facing the congregation in the new manner, the altar tends to create the appearance of an assembly that looks in on itself, and of a rite of communion between the participants. This loses much of the symbolic meaning of the previous orientation, in which the priest celebrates the Mysteries while facing God (the tabernacle and the cross) together with the faithful behind him, who beg the Lord to save and protect them.

We now stepped out of the church. It was eleven in the morning, and in the old Nürnberger Bratwurst Glöckl restaurant a number of workers were eating freshly-made *Weißwürste*, or soft white sausages (photos 3 and 4).

Gloria explained that I was witnessing a typical Bavarian scene and pointed out an interesting fact: that here, all the genuine local restaurants are frequented by everyone, regardless of social class. She went on to say that it was in this exact place that she met her husband, Prince Johannes von Thurn und Taxis, who, although already well on in years, was far from intimidated by this young woman; indeed, he correctly sensed that her fresh vitality was just what was needed to inject new vigour into an ancient family that was about to die out.

But let us return to the *Weißwürste*, which deserve a few words of their own, since they occupy an important place in the life of the inhabitants of this country and are thus eaten with a sort of reverence, and according to a precise ritual. Furthermore, I know for sure that the Pope has always been keen on them.

The ingredients and consistency of this speciality are unique and, from the Roman point of view, rather strange. These sausages are made almost entirely of veal, with bacon, salt, pepper and parsley added, the whole bound together in an egg base. They are eaten as soon as they are made, generally in mid-morning, and are served in a tureen, still floating in the hot water in which they were prepared, since they are not cooked, but just heated. They are eaten together with Brezen and sweet mustard, and must of course be washed down with a generous jug of beer.

The archbishop's palace

It was now time for a brief visit to the Fürstenried Park, where Ratzinger has enjoyed walking ever since he was at the seminary, and which he also liked to visit when he was the bishop of this city. In 1925 it was bought by the diocese, together with the princely residence – formerly a hunting lodge – that lies within its boundaries. During the Second World War, when the Georgianum diocesan seminary, which Ratzinger was attending, became too dangerous because of the air-raids, the students were moved here to Fürstenried, to continue, as best they could in those chaotic times, their lessons and their training for the priesthood.

Our tour then took us to the palace of the Archbishop of Munich, with its fine façade designed by Cuvilliés in 1733, and formerly the property of Count Holnstein, an illegitimate offspring of the Wittelsbach family. This is why the large coat of arms on the outside of the building has a red band running through it.

We were welcomed by Fr Rupert von Stolbert, the cardinal's amiable young secretary. On the ground floor we saw a charming late eighteenth-century wooden statue given by the then Cardinal Ratzinger, and which is often used in the procession on Palm Sunday. The statue is of Jesus riding an ass (photo 5).

The chapel is a bit further on. Here, a fine sixteenth-century wooden triptych hangs above the altar, and there is also a splendid Tyrolean lectern from the same school as the large crucifix on the first floor, in the ante-chamber to the main reception rooms. On the same wall there are two painted and gilded wooden statues of St Benno and St Corbinian.

Joseph Ratzinger was the first priest of the diocese in eighty years to be made head of the pastoral government of this large and ancient Bavarian diocese, which embraces two places: Munich and, as we will see, the nearby town of Freising.

When called to this post, the future Pope was a lecturer based in Regensburg, having previously taught theology at the universities of Bonn, Münster and Tübingen. He had accepted the chair of Theology and Dogma at Regensburg partly because the university there was more peaceful than many others, where student revolts were in full swing, and partly because this Bavarian town was also home to his brother Georg, who was director of the famous youth choir there (the Regensburger Domspatzen). Ratzinger had thus hoped to reunite his family and to live with his brother and his sister Maria; and as he said in his autobiography, the proposed promotion to the Archbishopric of Munich surprised him and also threw his life into some disorder. He would probably have preferred to carry on as an academic and lecturer, but the obedience that has been a hallmark of his life of course led him to accept.

Well before he became Pope, Ratzinger asked John Paul II more than once to relieve him of his duties as Prefect of the Congregation for the Doctrine of the Faith, so that he could return to Regensburg and continue his beloved studies; but the Pope always refused to lose such a valued colleague. And then, after the death of John Paul II, it was Providence, acting through the Sacred College of Cardinals, that elected to keep him in Rome definitively. This time too, no longer young yet still wishing to pursue his career as a theologian, Ratzinger immediately accepted the burdensome responsibility that the Church had placed on his shoulders.

But let us return to Munich, where Ratzinger was ordained a bishop on 28 May 1977. The motto that the young bishop chose, and was to keep when he became Pope, was *Cooperatores veritatis* ('Fellow-workers in the truth') – entirely suitable, granted the demands of the mission that lay ahead, and also his experience as a *peritus* to Josef Frings, the cardinal from Cologne, as well as his experience as a lecturer in various universities in Germany. He was all too aware of the difficulties that awaited him in this post, having already experienced the ferment that was shaking the Catholic world and that threatened to undermine the solidity of its faith; just as he was not blind to the dangers which, in this climate, now threatened Truth itself – which, when not actually denied, was smothered and confused by other partial and often insignificant truths.

Why is this attitude so common nowadays? Perhaps the concept of Truth is considered too huge for us human beings? Or perhaps – longing as we do for a freedom which we ill understand – we are afraid to be judged by Truth itself.

However, when Truth is absent, it is replaced in every heart by anguish, and everything seems to lose its meaning. Addressing this theme in a homily shortly before the conclave that elected him Pope, Ratzinger, then a senior cardinal, outlined the current situation of the Catholic faith with great lucidity: "How many doctrinal winds have we seen in these last two decades? How many ideological currents and changes in intellectual fashion! . . . From Marxism to liberalism and libertinism;

from collectivism to radical individualism; from atheism to a vague religious mysticism. . . . Whilst relativism – this is to say, allowing oneself to be carried here and there by any doctrinal wind – seems to be the only belief that is accepted today. We are creating a dictatorship of relativism that recognises nothing as definitive and whose only ultimate value is the individual and his wishes."

How could I fail to reflect on all these things as I was looking round this archbishop's palace which had been home to the future Pope and witness to his life and pastoral activities; this residence which had known his daily routines and had seen him at prayer? After all, this was one of the most promising and brilliant theologians in Germany, who during the Council opted decisively for progress, along with a group of determined colleagues; but who, being well balanced by nature and obedient towards the Holy Spirit, had a change of heart when he saw the danger inherent in a number of excessively radical positions.

Freising: the other part of the diocese

As I have said, the city of Munich is only one of two municipalities that make up the diocese. The other is Freising, a small town only a few miles away, and full of cafés and flower shops. Until 1802 the bishop's seat was here, but the forces of secularisation caused it to be moved to Munich, and the two dioceses were merged.

Joseph Ratzinger has a number of links to this town, all of which are important. It was here that he studied for the priesthood, before becoming a lecturer at the university and then returning as archbishop.

On the feastday of St Peter and St Paul in 1951, Joseph Ratzinger and his brother Georg, along with about forty other candidates, were ordained to the priesthood in the cathedral of Freising by Cardinal-Archbishop Faulhaber. This is how Ratzinger recalls the event in his autobiography: "It was a glorious sunny day which I will always remember as the most important in my life. One must not be superstitious, but just when the old archbishop laid his hands on my head, a bird – perhaps a lark – rose up from the high altar of the cathedral and sang a joyful song. I felt as though a voice from on high were saying that this was right, that I was on the right path."

Rereading these words today, I cannot help smiling happily and also reflecting that the Lord in Heaven really does have a plan for each and every one of us; nor does it matter what particular task is allotted to us. Obviously the Pope's mission is unique and singular, but we are all children of God, and thus loved and wanted. This leads me to reflect on the simplicity of heart of our Pope who, even as a young priest, was willing to read the signs – in this case the unexpected appearance of a lark – which Providence throws in our path, but which, blind and closed to the world as we are, we often do not see.

It was now time to start our visit. On top of the small hill of Domberg was the famous cathedral, surrounded by ancient buildings that once housed the town's university but now houses a library and an adult study centre. Originally Romanesque, this great sacred edifice was later remodelled in the Baroque style.

This overlaying of architectural styles is a typically Bavarian phenomenon, and one which we frequently came across during our travels. As in the church of St Emmeram in Regensburg, the frescos and stucco decorations in this cathedral were executed by the Asam brothers. Here in Freising, however, these two master artisans performed a real *tour de force*, completing the work in just one year, in time for the diocese to celebrate its millennium in 1724. The frescos on the ceiling and on the walls of the nave illustrate various episodes in the life of St Corbinian, who founded this diocese. And it is indeed a matter of record that the saintly bishop Corbinian came here some time in the eighth century.

We were lucky enough to see the inside of the cathedral free of the scaffolding that had covered it for the previous two years. The last major restoration had taken place in 1920. But now, a few days before the arrival of Benedict XVI, we were surprised by the sheer splendour of the place: the fifteenth-century choir stalls in dark oak; the eighteenth-century organ; and the huge stucco crucifix with the Madonna weeping at its feet. And then the crypt, where the bones of St Corbinian are kept in a golden reliquary.

The story of St Corbinian

The diocesan museum is very near the cathedral, and since it houses one of the world's largest collections of religious objects, we decided to visit it.

I was particularly struck by the expressive strength of the faces of the Madonna and Jesus in the fifteenth-century paintings of the South Tyrolean school: ancient in style, but at the same time so modern and realistic. It seems to me that some of the expressions on these faces perfectly reflect the state of mind of the age we live in.

In 1982, when Joseph Ratzinger was called to Rome by Pope John Paul II to become Prefect of the Congregation for the Doctrine of the Faith, as a farewell present he gave this museum a crucifixion painted in 1475 by the school of Freising.

We next searched out a painting that interested us greatly: the one by Jan Polak, showing St Corbinian and the bear (photo 6). According to the legend, a bear attacked and killed the saintly bishop's horse as he was riding to Rome. Corbinian reprimanded the bear and, as a punishment, made it carry to the Eternal City the baggage that the horse would otherwise have carried. However, having arrived in Rome, the saint let the bear go free.

We looked at the picture fondly. And now, as I write this, I cannot refrain from relating an episode that subsequently occurred beneath the Mariensäule in Munich, a few hours after Ratzinger arrived there as Benedict XVI. Referring to the famous story of Corbinian and the bear (which, incidentally, he put on his coat of arms), the Pope compared it to his own life; adding the following humorous comment: "In my case, Our Lord provided a different ending."

Several years before, he had written the following passage at the end of his autobiography: "The story goes that when he got to Rome, St Corbinian freed the bear. We are not told whether the beast then went off to Abruzzo or returned to the Alps. I carried my baggage to Rome and for several years have been walking round the streets of the Eternal City, still bearing this burden. I do not know when I will be let free, but I do know that the following words apply to me too: 'I have become thy beast of burden, and am thus near to thee.'"

Having arrived in Rome, the cardinal and future Pope was certainly not given the freedom that he perhaps hoped for at the bottom of his heart; indeed, the burden he carried was to become greater still.

The Wieskirche

In the town down below, the Marienplatz is the main square and is a miniature version of the one that carries the same name in Munich.

Before leaving Freising, we attended evening Mass in the church of St Peter and St Paul (photo 7), which Ratzinger often went to as a young seminarian. The last time he went there as a cardinal was on 1 January 2004, to celebrate the fiftieth anniversary of the priestly ordination of his fellow student Walter Brugger, today the chaplain of the Wieskirche (church in the meadow) in the nearby woods (photo 9).

There is a fine gold and silver altarpiece made by Ignaz

Günther in 1756, with silver statues of St Augustine and St Norbert on either side of it. The Mass was restrained; the faithful knelt to take communion and the final blessing was given with the Holy Sacrament.

A lady in the same pew as us recognised Gloria and once outside the church found an excuse to talk to her. Gloria told her that we were following in the footsteps of Benedict XVI, which is why we had come to Mass here. We said that we were keen not just to see the places that were dear to the Pope, but also to taste their atmosphere, and that we were now off to the Via Crucis in the nearby woods of which Joseph Ratzinger was, as we knew, so fond. Infected by our enthusiasm, the lady offered to show us the way, since it was not very easy to find.

The walk along a well-kept forest track takes about forty minutes. At intervals along the way, small edifices protect the painted stucco images of the Stations of the Cross (photo 8). Under eight of these is a series of meditations and prayers.

The sun was filtering through the leaves of the tall fir trees. Once in a while a bicyclist passed us, or a farmer on his tractor. At the end of the walk – and this seemed strange in a country as unfailingly well-organised as Germany – we had to cross a main road (the 301) with cars hurtling along it. If you are lucky enough to avoid getting run down, you then come to the Wieskirche, a small votive church that was built in the nineteenth century.

It was almost dark when Walter Brugger, the Pope's old friend from the seminary, opened the door to us. Once again, I found myself standing in front of a feast of stucco, columns and frescos, though all on a small scale. Above the altar is a picture, in a gold and silver frame, of Christ at the column of the flagellation (photo 10). The portrayal of the suffering Christ is powerful and penetrating, and the red of the column is the same as the red of the blood flowing from wounds on his pale body. Statues of the now familiar St Corbinian and of St Martin stand on either side of the altar; whilst display-cases containing old *ex voto* offerings made out of wax are arranged in a semi-circle around it.

In this church, buried in green woods and so silent and far from everything, the veil that separates us from the Mystery is almost transparent. It is easy to see why the future Pope was so fond of the place. Gloria and I said the Lord's Prayer, as we had decided we would do in all the churches we were to visit on our journey.

A trip to Maria Eck with Benedict XVI's friendly driver

The next day started in a curious way, with an appointment at ten in the morning in a rather unlikely place for two people on a pilgrimage of sorts. We were to go to the bank of Hauck & Aufhäuser, where we were due to meet with its director, Thaddäus Joseph Kühnel.

The riddle is easily explained, however. This reserved Bavarian had kindly offered to take us to the sanctuary of Maria Eck. This was a great honour, since for many years such treatment had been reserved exclusively for Joseph Ratzinger. Indeed, Thaddäus Kühnel had acted as driver – though of a rather special sort – to His Eminence in Bavaria.

While papers piled up on his desk, this devoted friend often left his duties as bank manager in order to drive the cardinal around. He made up for lost time by working at night. This did not bother him at all; what mattered was the chance of being in the company of this man of God.

"From the very first moment, I knew that this priest was special, and I came under his spell," he told us. "It was worth making any sacrifice in order to be able to spend a few hours with him." I also understood why a man such as Kühnel should appeal to Joseph Ratzinger: discreet in style and light of step, he walks silently and talks quietly.

We got into Thaddäus' comfortable Mercedes, with Gloria sitting in front and myself behind. In one of the back seat pockets I noticed a copy of *Salt of the Earth*, the famous interview with the then cardinal and a volume that was very important not only in my own journey towards faith, but also, I believe, in that of many others.

Herr Kühnel had met the three Ratzingers – Georg, Maria and Joseph – in August 1978, at the convent of Adelholzen. This was only a few hundred yards away from Villa Auli, the holiday residence of the Archbishop of Munich and Freising, and it was here that Ratzinger used to spend his summers.

As we drove along, Kühnel took us into his confidence. "When we were in the car we used to entrust ourselves to the protection of St Christopher," he said, "and then we would always recite the rosary and sing songs in honour of Mary. When the cardinal was called to Rome in 1982, I told him not to worry and that I would take him all the Bavarian things that he was so fond of. So from his first year there, and every year after that, I drove down with the Advent crown, *Weißwürste*, fruit and a Christmas tree. Sometimes I also took a few bottles of his favourite water." I was moved by such simple generosity, but at this stage curiosity got the better of me and I interrupted him to ask what water he meant. "Well, the water from Adelholzener Primusquelle. That's the spring of the Roman legionary Primus, who was martyred in the same place where there's now a small fountain."

Obviously, we asked Kühnel to stop at this famous fountain (photo 14) so that we could taste the cardinal's favourite water. Dozens of people were queuing in front of us, waiting to fill up the plastic bottles they had brought, whilst in the nearby valley we could glimpse the large buildings of the Adelholzener bottling plant, which produces fifty million bottles of mineral water every day. There could hardly have been a greater contrast between this and the sight of people leaning over Primus' fountain.

We continued on our trip, driving through thick woods from which we emerged into hills covered with green meadows. By the side of the road to the sanctuary there were a number of small stations containing sacred images as an invitation to meditation. According to the tradition of pilgrimages, the idea of *statio*, or rest, is indissolubly linked to that of *commotio*, or motion. On the third Sunday of May, the sanctuary celebrates its feast day with a solemn procession attended by the faithful wearing traditional costumes.

When we arrived at Maria Eck (photo 11), I was surprised to see that the church is a miniature version of the basilica of Santa Maria Maggiore in Rome. We went inside. Above the main altar is the famous painting of the Madonna and child, here with curly blond locks, surrounded by kneeling worshippers, one of whom is a Benedictine monk. Some claim that this might be the abbot of the nearby monastery of Seeon, since it was he who first encouraged pilgrimages to this spot. A white lamb with a candle on either side rests on a small shelf at the foot of the painting, whilst above it are two figures in gilded wood – the Father and the Son – with the dove of the Holy Ghost above; appropriately enough, since the Holy Trinity is worshipped in this immensely charming and mysterious sacred place.

The church was built in 1626 by Benedictine monks. According to legend, a group of peasants saw an apparition consisting of three lights in the middle of the fields, and immediately built an altar, followed by a second and a third on each side. Thus the name *Eck*, meaning corner.

Outside the church is a terrace with a breath-taking view over Lake Chiemsee, which is also known as the Lake of the Peasants. Thaddäus informed me that the two other great Bavarian lakes are Starnberg – which, having attracted numerous sovereigns over the centuries, is called the Lake of the Kings – and Tegernsee, much favoured by the upper bourgeoisie as a holiday resort.

In the small external portico, on the other hand, numerous wooden pilgrims' crosses are stacked up against the wall. Some have a request for a grace written on them; whilst others were given in recognition of grace already granted. This is a Bavarian tradition which we were also to come across at Altötting.

At the cardinal's dinner table

We then had a brief lunch break in the monastery's restaurant (photo 12).

Herr Kühnel had kindly reserved the same table at which Ratzinger had always dined, and at which he had often celebrated his birthday. It was in a corner, with a 180° view over the valley.

Like an experienced host, Brother Eric did the rounds of the tables, greeting the diners, asking the odd question, smiling and chatting politely, but preferring not to sit down with his guests. It was he who successfully set up and managed the restaurant and the small hotel, which almost never has any vacancies, being fully booked by a faithful clientele that returns every year.

Very much in passing, perhaps for fear of being indiscreet, he mentioned that Joseph Ratzinger had last come here in May 2004. He was, however, more forthcoming about another fond memory: the unforgettable eightieth birthday party for Father Ignatius, a Franciscan friar who had heard confessions for thirty years at St Peter's in Rome. He is now buried in the cemetery of the convent where he was chaplain in the summer months.

The two Ratzinger brothers often came to this sanctuary. Sometimes Herbert von Karajan would be at the table next to theirs, enjoying the peace of Maria Eck after conducting a concert in Salzburg.

On the journey home I spotted a small church with a typical onion-domed bell-tower. Thaddäus told me that every now and then on their journeys, the cardinal would point through the car window to some small church along the way, proudly announcing that such-and-such a style was only to be found in Bavaria. I asked Thaddäus what he thought Ratzinger loved the most about Bavaria. "The nature, the mountains and the countryside," came the unequivocal reply. "Often, on the spur of the moment, we used to stop off at these small sacred places which are the true beating hearts of villages that are unknown to the public at large. We used to light a candle and recite a Hail Mary."

As we drove on, I looked around, enjoying the sensuous character of these spots. What with the woods, the mountain tops, the green hills and the farm animals roaming freely, the wonder of creation made itself felt with particular power.

I was reminded of a passage in one of Ratzinger's sermons: "God's creation was not entrusted to us to be exploited, but to be protected with deep reverence and made into a divine garden in which humans can live full lives."

The abbey of Scheyern — an oasis of peace and prayer

One other destination awaited us before we turned our attention to the places that the Pope had known in his childhood and youth: the abbey of Scheyern, where Ratzinger often went for rest and meditation. Its convenient position halfway between Munich and Regensburg, as well as its large gardens and the nearby woods, can only have added to its appeal for the future Pope.

Immediately after he was made Archbishop of Munich and Freising in 1977, he came here for the feast of the Holy Cross. Since then he has returned to Scheyern twenty-three times, most recently for the feast of Pentecost in 2003. His duties kept him elsewhere in 2004; and having confirmed his intention to return here in 2005, he was then elected Pope at the conclave in the Sistine Chapel.

We were held up by heavy traffic on the motorway, from which we had nevertheless been able to admire large expanses of well-kept hop fields: as we have already seen, this is a vital ingredient in the beer-making process.

As God willed, we finally drove into one of the white and yellow courtyards of this impressive monastery built around an old castle belonging to the counts of Scheyern, who in 1115 moved to he nearby village of Wittelsbach, home to the famous dynasty that has played such an important role in the history of Bavaria.

The abbot (photo 15) was waiting for us outside the door, and looked distinctly irritated, evidently because we were late. Summing up our courage, we apologised politely. However, he seemed to be a man with little time for small talk, and took us straight to the chapel, where the small community of monks was already in choir, ready to sing the Angelus.

The organ was played by an old lady, and German hymns followed litanies in Gregorian chant. It took us only a few minutes to be transported into another world and to sense our closeness to all that is mysterious and sacred.

I began to experience that same sense of peace that I feel in the convent of Rosano, near Florence, whenever I go and see the Benedictine nuns there. I am always reminded, too, that this place of which I am so fond was also a favourite of Cardinal Ratzinger's after he moved to Rome. Most of all, he liked to spend the feast of Corpus Christi here. Among their various activities, these nuns, to whom the Pope is linked by numerous ties, make ecclesiastical vestments, formerly for Pope John Paul II and now for Pope Benedict XVI.

Looking around and breathing in the atmosphere, I began to understand all the more clearly why the then cardinal so much liked coming here. It must have been a breath of fresh air and a complete break from the great responsibilities and numerous duties that filled his days in unremitting succession, first as Archbishop of Munich, and then as Prefect of the former Holy Office.

When you walk through the doors of this ancient monastery, you leave behind all the cares of the world. To illustrate the idea, I will allow myself to use a modest – but, I think, effective – image. It seems to me that when you enter a place like this, the same process takes place as when you pour broth through a sieve: the waste matter is too big to get through the small holes, and so stays in the sieve, ready to be thrown away. I have the impression that the same thing happens to the soul, which is, as it were, filtered and purified by prayer and reflection, becoming more lucid and better able to appreciate its own limits and to ask the Holy Spirit for renewed strength.

In this monastery the days are governed by rules that are quite different from the ones that apply in the world outside, and with the rhythm of *ora et labora*, of prayer alternating with work, time flies by in a way that is both more Christian and more human. To quote the rule formulated by St Benedict, holy monk and father of Europe: "The Lord always comes before everything else."

The abbot then showed us around. Marching along the long white corridors, he pointed out the various transformations and reconstructions that the abbey has undergone over the centuries, and which are still clearly visible. We now learned that for nineteen years this monk had also acted as parish priest in the small villages nearby, which between them were home to about six thousand souls.

On one of the walls I noticed a small plaque in memory of a certain Father Joseph, and asked who he was. The abbot told us that at the beginning of the twentieth century a number of monks were sent to America. Father Joseph was among them, and died at the age of 42: he was one of the passengers who went down with the Titanic.

Then we went into a small dining room and sat down to eat with the small community of thirteen monks.

When I asked the abbot how many square metres of floor space there was in the monastery, he said he only knew how many windows it had: eight hundred.

Father Andrea was the most talkative person in the group, and told us about the school they run in the monastery and that it is attended by about three hundred pupils every year. They aim to educate people who started work at an early age and were therefore unable to get their school certificate.

For some time now, the monastery has also had an 'open day' that attracts many people who come along to look round and to find out about the monastic way of life. This imaginative initiative has thankfully eliminated many of the prejudices that the secular world holds against those whose lives are dedicated entirely to God. Indeed, some have even discovered a religious vocation. Brother Andrea is an example of someone with a college education who came along for the day in order to see Benedictine spirituality at work, and decided to stay.

Looking through the large visitors' book on a table in the sitting room near the dining area, I recognised the unmistakable handwriting – small and firm – of Joseph Ratzinger.

The following words were above his signature: "Thank you for the peace that comes from listening to the word of the Lord in this community dedicated to serving God."

There was still a bit more time, after the meal, to get a closer look at the marvels inside these sacred walls.

In the large Romanesque church that was built in 1215 and remodelled in the Baroque style in 1769, there is a series of eighteen frescos depicting the life of St Benedict. These were executed in 1923. Golden statues of St Benedict and his twin sister Scolastica, who like her brother gave her life to God, stand on the high altar; whereas a relic from the Holy Cross is housed in a side-chapel. Here, in a reliary case with a clear glass front that renders its contents visible to worshippers, is kept a gem-encrusted golden cross inside which is an 18-centimetre-long relic from the True Cross.

The splendid seventeenth-century sacristy with its decorations in carved wood was made by a craftsman from Augsburg and houses valuable reliquaries made with enamel, silver, gold and precious stones. The abbot also showed us various copies of the Gospels transcribed by monks over the centuries, and which are kept in a library containing one hundred thousand volumes (photo 16). It was interesting to see how tradition keeps on evolving, so that where work is concerned, the rules governing life in the abbey have been rewritten to take account of the appearance of modern inventions such as the tractor, the bicycle and the motorcycle.

During the days of rest and spiritual retreat at Scheyern, Joseph Ratzinger often joined the resident community for prayer and meals, and otherwise spent his time reading and going for long walks in the woods. "Here, there was no-one demanding his attention, and he enjoyed complete peace," said the abbot. "Sometimes he took Mass alone. This was because he liked to worship every morning in a Gothic chapel where a tabernacle in the shape of a dove hung from the ceiling, directly above the altar." I can easily see how the fruitful meditation that took place here provided inspiration for the cardinal's theological studies and pastoral activities.

There is also a lesson for the rest of us in the desire of the future Pope to retreat whenever he could into silence and prayer. Although his responsibilities have always been far greater than ours, each one of us nevertheless has a duty to operate effectively in the circumstances in which we find ourselves; and thus, to stay as close to God as possible. This might involve spending

1. *With its famous onion-domed twin towers, the Frauenkirche is Munich's most famous landmark.*

2. *Marienplatz in Munich: the statue of Mary and the ancient musical clock on the face of the town hall.*

3. *A lunch-break in Munich: beer, Weißwürste and Brezen.*

4. *A young waitress dressed in traditional costume in the famous Nürnberger Bratwurst Glöckl restaurant in Munich.*

5. *Statue on the ground floor of the palace of the Archbishop of Munich and Freising, given by the then Cardinal Ratzinger before he was transferred to Rome.*

6. *St Corbinian and the bear, painted by Jan Polak in 1489, now in the diocesan museum near Freising cathedral.*

7. *The interior of the church of St Peter and St Paul in the centre of Freising. As a young student at the seminary, Joseph Ratzinger was very fond of this place.*

8. *One of the Stations of the Cross in the woods near Freising.*

9. *The Wieskirche at the end of the Via Crucis in the woods near Freising.*

10. *Christ at the column of the flagellation, by Johann Jäger, in a gold and silver frame. This small and exquisite painting, dated 1745, is in the Wieskirche.*

11. *The church in the charming Marian sanctuary of Maria Eck.*

12. *Thaddäus Kühnel, Gloria von Thurn und Taxis, Brother Eric and myself in front of the restaurant at Maria Eck.*

13. Wooden crosses – some of them ex voto left by pilgrims in the portico at Maria Eck, left here by pilgrims. Some are ex voto, whilst others are thanks for graces already granted. The same tradition is to be found at Altötting.

14. The fountain of the Roman legionary Primus and source of Joseph Ratzinger's favourite water.

15. The abbot of the monastery of Scheyern.

16. *Produced by the monks at Scheyern, this volume describes life in a monastery today.*

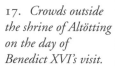

17. *Crowds outside the shrine of Altötting on the day of Benedict XVI's visit.*

18. *Ex voto offerings in the portico outside the famous Chapel of Mercy in Altötting.*

19. *Lunette above the entrance to the Chapel of Mercy in Altötting, showing the Madonna dressed in red.*

20. *Inside the Chapel of Mercy: the sumptuous gold and silver altarpiece which frames the statue of the Madonna of Mercy.*

21. *A copy of the Altöttinger Liebfrau-enbote, the shrine's journal, to which the Holy Father still subscribes.*

22. *A typical stretch of countryside in the Holy Father's native land.*

23. *One of the many wayside crucifixes along the roads in Lower Bavaria.*

24. *A typical shrine surrounded by farmland.*

25. *Churches surrounded by just a few houses are a typical feature of the Bavarian countryside.*

26. *Marktl am Inn, the native town of Joseph Ratzinger.*

27. *Gloria von Thurn und Taxis; Hubert Gschwendtner, the mayor of Marktl am Inn; and myself.*

28. *Inside one of the Bäckereien on the main street of Marktl am Inn.*

29. *Cardboard packaging for buns in the shape of a mitre, along with beer jugs, candles, cups and bottles of beer bearing the image of the Pope.*

30. *The marble font in which Joseph Ratzinger was baptised in the parish church of St Oswald. Behind it is the neo-Gothic triptych which was formerly above the high altar.*

31. *A group of altar servers waits for the Holy Father to arrive in his native town.*

32. *Gloria and I with the Pope among the crowds in Marktl am Inn. The lady with short hair and a white shirt is the mayoress of Wadowice, where Pope John Paul II was born.*

33. *Brightly painted buildings in the main square of Tittmoning.*

34. *The church of St Oswald in Traunstein, where Joseph and Georg Ratzinger celebrated their first Masses.*

35. *The farmhouse in which the Ratzinger family lived from 1937 to 1951. Built in 1726, it lies in the village of Hufschlag just outside Traunstein. It is still surrounded by fruit trees.*

36. *A view of the picturesque Monastery of Au am Inn.*

37. *The church of St Peter (Peterskirche) off the road between Au and Aschau am Inn is one of Bavaria's few churches built on a circular plan.*

38. *The members of Regensburg's Marian Congregation for Women with the bishop, Monsignor Gerhard Ludwig Müller, in front of the cathedral.*

39. *The Alte Kapelle in Regensburg, which Benedict XVI visited during his apostolic journey to Bavaria.*

40. *The courtyard of the Schloss St Emmeram, the residence of the Thurn und Taxis family in Regensburg, with the famous fountain of the prince electors in front of it.*

41. *Inside the Schloss St Emmeram with the Meister Georg Ratzinger.*

42. *Joseph Ratzinger's house in Pentling, a village on the outskirts of Regensburg.*

44. *Chico, a friend of the Pope's, in the garden of Benedict XVI's house in Pentling.*

43. *The wall calendar in the Pope's house is still frozen at Friday 7 January 2005, the last time when Ratzinger slept here.*

45. *Agnes Heindl, Gloria von Thurn und Taxis and myself pose by the prie-dieu in the chapel in the Pope's house.*

46. *An audience with the Holy Father in the seminary in Regensburg.*

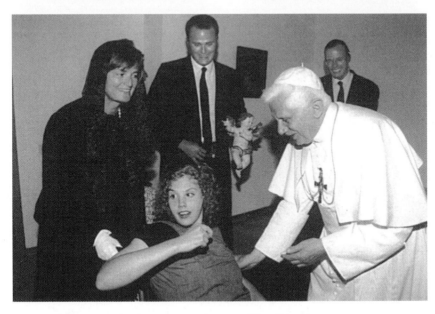

47. *Gloria von Thurn und Taxis with her niece Pilar Flick in the wheelchair. Albert von Thurn und Taxis is holding the small guardian angel that he is about to give to the Holy Father.*

a moment of rest and reflection in the company of people like monks whose spiritual values can help and sustain us.

As the hours passed, the abbot opened up increasingly, revealing himself to be, among other things, a marvellous host. And as we got to know each other, this man of few words with his left eyebrow raised in disapproval turned out to be the most charming and welcoming of monks.

When the time came to leave, I gave the abbot a white and yellow flag with the Pope's coat of arms on it. As he stood there waving us a warm goodbye with one hand and happily brandishing the flag with the other, it was as though he were a child.

IV

ALTÖTTING – HOME TO
THE MADONNA

"Mary has helped us"

Having left Munich and Freising, and now on our way towards
the scenes of Ratzinger's childhood and youth, we decided to
stop off in a place that we knew to be close to the heart of the
Pope and also of all Bavarians.

The shrine of Altötting is the most important Marian
sanctuary in Bavaria – the equivalent, say, of Czestochowa for
the Poles and Pope John Paul II.

For over 1,250 years, this small town half way between
Munich and Salzburg, four hundred metres above sea level in
the famous foothills of the Bavarian Alps, and surrounded by
the magical woods of Holzland, has been the spiritual capital
of Bavaria.

The story of the Chapel of Mercy and the black octagon at
its heart in which the statue of the Madonna is kept, can be
summed up in four words: "Mary has helped us". However, the
fame of Altötting was established long ago.

It all began when the Madonna cured two children in two
separate miracles. After that, the pilgrimages started and
people began to come here with their troubles, praying for the

miraculous intervention of the Virgin Mary. Many left tangible evidence of their gratitude; indeed, the portico outside the shrine is covered with small framed illustrations of the cures granted to the faithful (photo 18). The oldest of these *ex voto* offerings dates back to 1501. However, the statue, 64 centimetres high and made of dark lime wood, was already inside the existing octagon around the year 1300, and in later centuries was framed by a sumptuous gold and silver altarpiece.

The Bavarians have always felt a strong bond with the Virgin Mary, so much so that the Wittelsbach family, which ruled here from 1180, dedicated themselves and their country to the Madonna of Altötting, even leaving instructions that when they died, their hearts should be placed in urns which were to be left permanently near the statue of their holy patroness.

Even though this beautiful town attracts about one million pilgrims every year, it is still a stranger to mass tourism and still unknown to the Italian tourists. When Gloria and I went there, the owners of the small and immaculately kept religious souvenir shops near the main square were getting ready for the crowds which would inevitably be attracted by the arrival of a Bavarian Pope known to be deeply attached to this shrine (photo 17). Many were also learning Italian, since Italy is the country which produces the highest number of pilgrims. I confess that I am proud of this.

A typical Bavarian couple

In Altötting we were the guests of Herr Krauss and his wife, friends of Gloria's mother. He is a maths teacher, tall and well-built, but wears a permanently thoughtful expression. She is an interior designer, short and energetic, and always attentive and enquiring.

The Krauss couple unfailingly wear traditional Tyrolean clothes and, as devout Catholics, they like to recite the rosary with their guests. Furthermore, their suitcases are always at the ready for the next pilgrimage.

Just a few months before our arrival, they had moved into a lovely first-floor flat above Anton Braun Müller's well-known shop selling religious articles right on the famous Kapellplatz. On the corner of the house to one side, there is a large statue of St Joseph and the Child. You often see these statues in Bavaria.

From the seven windows of this light-filled flat you can keep an eye on everything that is going on around the Chapel of Mercy. An old *prie-dieu* is placed in a prominent position in the main sitting room for the benefit of anyone wishing to pray while looking directly onto the holy octagonal chapel.

The Krausses are warm and generous hosts, and on their kitchen table there is always something to eat. The one daily appointment we were expected to keep was for *Brotzeit*, the first meal of the day and one that is something of a rite, in which the whole family gathers round the table to talk and spend time together; and the various types of bread and large choice of hams, cheeses and sausages were a temptation that I could not resist.

We went outside to stretch our legs. The main square was full of people, with customers sipping beer in the bars while numerous pilgrims with wooden crosses on their shoulders were heading towards the Chapel of Mercy, where the crosses would be left in the portico.

We reached the Hotel Post, whose owner Gerhard Tandler, a former Minister of the Interior, is a friend of Gloria's. He was most happy to see us and immediately sat down to talk. Inevitably, the conversation turned to Joseph Ratzinger, and Tandler told us about the time he came here anonymously with his brother Georg: "After Mass, they came to the Hotel Post and ate freshly-made *Brezen* and *Weißwürste* with *Weißwurstsenf* (sweet mustard)."

Not far from the hotel is the Panorama, one of the town's main attractions. Having bought your ticket, you go along a long dark corridor and up the twenty-three steps of a creaking staircase, before emerging into a large round room with a floor space of about 1,000 square metres. The walls, covered in frescos executed by Gebhard Fugel in 1903, depict the day of the crucifixion of Christ in Jerusalem. In order to recreate the right atmosphere, Fugel apparently went to Palestine to see the sites and get a feel for them.

Georg Ratzinger once said that although he had studied Fugel at school, it was "only as adults" that he and his brother first visited the Panorama. Even in this age of special effects, I was impressed by the way that you are immediately transported back 2,000 years and feel as though you are witnessing real events.

A mysterious darkness, full of light

What, though, is the Pope's relationship with the holy town of Altötting?

From childhood onwards, the young Joseph used to come here with his parents; and in the years to come, numerous public and private occasions brought him back here to kneel at the feet of the Madonna in the Chapel of Mercy. The last time had been in January 2005, when he and his brother Georg came here on a private pilgrimage, only a few months before he then became Pope Benedict XVI.

It was on that occasion that he put his name to the preface to a new guidebook which is now a collector's item: "I had the good fortune to be born near Altötting," he wrote, "and pilgrimages here with my family are among the happiest of my childhood. Naturally, for me the highlight of these journeys was always the Chapel of Mercy with its mysterious darkness and the Most Holy Black Madonna in her precious robes. . . ." (photo 20).

I have chosen the following episode from the many reminiscences of the then cardinal: "I have a very clear memory of one of my visits to Altötting. It was a cold day and I was crossing the large square, heading towards the famous chapel. The restricted space inside was overcrowded. Candles were burning everywhere in the semi-darkness. The chapel was filled almost exclusively with women praying and singing Marian hymns. I sensed that this was a way not just to overcome my weaknesses, but also to find renewed strength."

I, too, now wished to visit this holy place. But before entering the most intimate heart of the chapel to kneel at the feet of the statue of the Madonna, I decided to pause behind a metal grille to the right of the vestibule; a position from which it is all the more moving to observe those at prayer.

On entering the very heart of the shrine, the pilgrim becomes part of the Mystery. From my viewpoint, on the other hand, I was able to admire the Mystery. As my eyes searched out every small gesture on the part of the worshippers, my heart beat hard.

In order to venerate the Madonna, you have to go through a small door above which is a lunette showing the Virgin dressed in red, her arms spread out to hold up a large blue mantle that protects the people of God who are kneeling at her feet (photo 19).

As soon as he was elected Pope, Ratzinger stated that Altötting was "the heart of Bavaria and one of the hearts of Europe." It is indeed true that together with Lourdes, Fatima, Czestochowa and Loreto, this tiny but splendid and ancient shrine is one of the five most important in Europe; so much so that in November 1980 it was visited by Pope John Paul II, who was accompanied, among other people, by Joseph Ratzinger, the then Archbishop of Munich and Freising. This event is recorded by a bronze statue by Leo Mol which is placed in a prominent position in the square.

Ratzinger has paid a number of visits to Altötting. In the Jubilee year of 1989 he celebrated the official Mass for the opening of the basilica of St Anne, which was needed to accommodate the increasing numbers of pilgrims. Ten years afterwards, in 1999, he returned to the same place to give an address to mark the 400th anniversary off the Marian Congregation of Men, which is attached to this shrine which is so close to the Pope's heart. Then in 2001 he joined thousands of pilgrims on the last leg of their journey as they walked from Regensburg to Altötting.

However, perhaps one of the most important memories of Ratzinger's life is the canonisation, which took place during his childhood, of Brother Conrad Parzham, the Capuchin porter of the shrine of Altötting.

The Pope's devotion to the Madonna is well known. Do not let us forget that immediately after his election, the first words spoken by Benedict XVI from the loggia at the front of St Peter's, were: "Rejoicing in the Lord who has arisen, and trusting in His lasting help, let us proceed. The Lord will help us and His Most Holy Mother Mary is with us."

Like his beloved predecessor John Paul II, Joseph Ratzinger has strong Marian loyalties. As he has said, "Mary is the expression of our closeness to God . . . it is moving to think that the Son of God should have a human mother to whom all of us are entrusted." And as the Pope himself has said, his relationship with the Holy Virgin has become more important over the years: "The older I get, the more dear and important the Mother of God becomes to me."

Years before this, Ratzinger had written the following words in a book entitled *Rapporto sulla fede*, published in English as *The Ratzinger Report*: "When I was a young theologian before the Second Vatican Council, I had a number of reservations about certain ancient formulas such as the famous one stating that one can never say enough about the Virgin Mary. I thought this excessive. . . . But now, in this confused period in which every sort of heretical deviation seems to be pressing against the doors of the true faith, I appreciate that these were not devout exaggerations, but rather a series of truths that are more valid today than ever before. . . . Indeed, if we wish to return to the truth concerning Jesus Christ, the Church, and man, then we must return to the Virgin Mary. . . . More than ever, the Madonna must be the *pedagogia* for teaching the Gospel to man today."

V

THE SCENES OF HIS CHILDHOOD AND EARLY YOUTH

It all began at Marktl am Inn

Still based in Altötting, where we continued to enjoy the generous hospitality of Herr Krauss and his wife, we planned to spend the next days visiting the scenes of the childhood and youth of Benedict XVI. We began with his birthplace: the town of Marktl am Inn (photo 26).

The bridge over the gently-sloping banks of the river; the bell-tower of the only church; the thick woods all around – such are the defining characteristics of this small town on the Inn, a major river which flows from its source in the Bavarian Alps until it joins the great Danube at Passau.

On the main road only a few paces away from the house where Joseph Ratzinger was born, we saw no fewer than three *Bäckereien* (bakeries) right next door to each other (photo 28). We parked the car and got out to go for a stroll.

A woman came up to greet us, smiling broadly. Prominently displayed in one of the shop windows was a well-known saying of the Pope's: "Those who believe are never alone." This aroused our curiosity, so we went in to have a cup of coffee.

The proprietress, Frau Leukert, told us that for the previous six months a constant flow of people had been following the so-called 'trail of Benedict'. We asked what this was. The Bavarian tourist office had wasted no time, came the answer. No sooner had a citizen of this country been elected to the throne of St Peter, than they created an itinerary about 200 miles long that took in the places linked with the Holy Father.

Ever since then, numerous pilgrims had been arriving, map in hand – some on foot with rucksacks on their backs; others on bicycles; and others travelling by car. "We used to be a small town in the back of beyond, but now the whole world is coming to our doors," this young Bavarian woman announced proudly from behind the counter of her shop.

There was a constant flow of people coming and going, so the bakery must have been the main place for the town's inhabitants to meet for a morning gossip. The packaging for the buns had been redesigned in the shape of a papal mitre, since when business had apparently doubled (photo 29).

A bit further on, we came to Marktplatz, where a plaque outside number 11 announces that Joseph Ratzinger was born in this house. A group of tourists were posing for a photograph, causing cars to screech to a halt, since the house is right near the turning off the main road.

"I was born on 16 April 1927, on Holy Saturday," wrote Ratzinger in his autobiography. "My family often commented on the fact that this was the last day of Holy Week and the day before Easter Sunday. I was baptised on the morning of the day after my birth, with water that had just been blessed the night before. That I was the first to be baptised with fresh holy water was an important sign." I like to reflect that in the first year of the pontificate of Benedict XVI, the 16 April was again an important date from the liturgical point of view – indeed, the most important, being Easter Day. It certainly seems that from the very start of his life, the Holy Father has enjoyed special protection from on high.

The baptism took place in the church of St Oswald. Today a new altar in white marble stands in the nave in the modern fashion, whereas the neo-Gothic wooden triptych that used to be above the high altar is now in the side-chapel on the left (photo 30).

In front of the triptych stands the now famous font, made out of white marble with angels carved all round it. A sweet-smelling white rose stood in a small glass vase at its base.

For the last ten years, Hubert Gschwendtner (photo 27) has been the town's mayor, combining this position with his job as a teacher at the local primary school. This charming and enterprising middle-aged man, who speaks perfect English, had the excellent idea of twinning Marktl am Inn with Wadowice, the home town of Pope John Paul II.

With the help of a young manager in a major local bank, Gschwendtner intends to turn Marktl into a spiritual destination, perhaps setting up a centre for studying the life, thought, and teachings of the town's most illustrious citizen. The mayor objects to the idea that the only things on offer should be an assortment of items bearing an image of the Pope, like beer, sausages and packets of sweet and savoury buns. Gloria and I wished him all success in his venture, but feared that the proverbial business acumen of his fellow-countrymen would provide stiff competition; although, that said, among the places we visited on our journey, Marktl was certainly the most efficiently organised.

It brought a smile to my face, but also moved me, to witness this strong urge on the part of the inhabitants to inform all-comers that this town on the banks of the river Inn really had been the scene of an event that to them seemed unimaginable – the birth of a future Pope. Benedict XVI is not, however, the first Pope to visit Marktl, since Pius VI stopped there for a meal on his way from Munich to Vienna in 1782.

Apart from having its own brewery, almost every small town in Bavaria also has a museum in honour of the homeland: another sign of the fundamental importance, even today, of cultural roots. The curator of the museum in Marktl is a busy amateur collector, and it was he who saved the font when the church of St Oswald was re-ordered in 1965. As a token of gratitude, His Holiness sent the museum a skullcap of his and a gold chalice engraved with the papal insignia.

It was strange to learn that on the other side of the river from Marktl am Inn, where the Pope was born on 16 April 1927, and almost directly opposite it, lay the town of Braunau am Inn, which witnessed the birth, on 20 April 1889, of another famous figure, though of the very opposite nature to the Pope: the satanic Adolf Hitler.

A few miles apart, therefore, and with an interval of about forty years, the births took place first of the man who gave the twentieth century one of the cruellest and most bloody ideologies in history, and then of a gentle and sensitive man who from his youth onwards dedicated his whole life to the service of God and his brothers.

Indeed, the Pope witnessed every stage of Nazism from its early beginnings to its collapse when Germany lost the Second World War. In one of his autobiographical works he recounts how first as a child and then later on, he saw the birth and then the spread of this new and terrible ideology. The 'paganisation' of society that came with it, and the ever-increasing pressure to conform, created serious problems for Ratzinger's father, who was a policeman, as well as for anyone who was not an active sympathiser.

The young Joseph Ratzinger, then a seminarian, was directly involved in the last years of the war, first with the anti-aircraft batteries in Munich, like his contemporaries, and then in a work camp.

Some have insinuated that these two activities suggest that the young man who was later to become Pope supported the Nazis. But these voices have been silenced by the absence of any evidence to support such claims. Not only did the young seminarian refuse to enrol as a volunteer, but he also extricated himself as soon as he could from the wartime duties that had been forced on him; and it was only after a long march and a period in a American POW camp that he was able to return home for good. Nourished by a faith that even then was mature, his Christian outlook ensured that he was quite capable of judging the facts for himself and of making his choices with lucidity.

Two entirely different stories, therefore, for two men born a few decades apart in two towns opposite each other on the same river Inn. The first has been compared to the Devil, whilst the second now guides the Church among the challenges of the modern world.

In between the two of them came John Paul II. He also suffered first hand experience of Nazism in his native Poland, before ending up under a communist regime that was no less ferocious. It is interesting, I think, to consider the coincidences. In the face of the evil figure of Adolf Hitler, who among other things was intent on levelling and weakening the Catholic Church, Providence produced two great men of faith who had known of him at first hand, who had suffered because of him, but whose experiences had given them an even more solid and profound belief in the beauty and value of the Christian Truth. In this too, the Pope and the man whom he always calls 'my beloved predecessor' seem to have shared the same destiny.

During his visit to Bavaria, Benedict XVI found space in his busy diary to spend a couple of hours in his home town. Gloria and I also went back there for the occasion. I must say that it is difficult to find words to describe the atmosphere among the crowds waiting for the Pope to arrive. It was like in some fairy-tale in which the inhabitants of a town have fallen under a benign spell.

The Pope, who has a tender heart, was visibly moved, too. After prayers in the church of St Oswald, he was due to meet just a few local notables, but was then carried away by the enthusiastic chanting and went on a spontaneous walkabout.

Gloria and I had intended to mix with the crowds and wait for the Pope anonymously. However, Providence arranged things otherwise. The mayor, whom we had met only a few weeks previously, invited us to sit in the seats that had been reserved for him; because, as he explained, he and his wife would have to be on their feet to greet the Holy Father and show him round.

Happily surprised by such kindness, we immediately sat down in our places behind the metal barriers on the main street of the town. The mayoress of Wadowice was sitting nearby. An attractive young woman with elegantly cut, short black hair and large dark eyes, she wore a smart white shirt and a large silver chain of office.

On the other side of the street from us was a group of altar servers in their cassocks (photo 31). This should not come as a surprise, since in Bavaria it is quite normal to serve Mass in this way, and is also considered an honour. Later, at the large outdoor Mass on Islinger Feld in Regensburg, no fewer than fifteen thousand young altar servers felt honoured to serve the liturgy of the Church in the person of Pope Benedict XVI. Even Prince Albert von Thurn und Taxis, Gloria's son and the heir to the family fortune, is still an altar server, in spite of the fact that he is no longer a boy.

When, to the accompaniment of chanting, music and waving, Joseph Ratzinger arrived in Marktl as Pope, he looked very happy; and, relaxed and at ease, he stopped here and there to greet people in the crowds eager to show the admiration and affection they felt for him. Entirely unexpectedly, he also paused to greet us (photo 32). I enthusiastically told him how much I had been struck by the beauty of his land. Kind as always, he nodded and thanked me.

Tittmoning – the town that the Pope dreamed of as a child

Early the next day we left Marktl and set out for Tittmoning. The road took us into the heart of the beautiful countryside that the Pope loves so much – meadows of a deep green that we Romans know only from the felt-tipped pens used by children; small hamlets and churches; and monasteries, mountains and forests.

As Ratzinger has written: "Tittmoning is the town that I dreamed of as a child."

There are two ancient entrances to the main square, one coming from Laufen and the other from Burghausen. The square is surrounded by grand old buildings in a style similar to that seen not far off in Salzburg, and the facade of the town hall is decorated with medallions bearing portraits of Roman emperors. The overall result is a fabulous interplay of colours: ochre, yellow, pink, green, sky blue and ivory (photo 33). Good taste and harmony are to be found throughout Bavaria.

We sat down in a café in front of which there was a large statue of the Virgin Mary. Nearby, at number 39 on the main square, our attention was drawn to the residence where the Ratzinger family lived from 1929 to 1933 and which today houses the Sparkasse bank.

The words *Gloria in excelsis Deo atque in terra pax* still run along the cornice on the façade in huge letters. In Wagnergasse, a small street to one side of the building, is a plaque announcing that this place was once home to an illustrious figure who was to become Pope. However, the cars parked close to the wall were almost blocking it from sight, and some children had expressed their disapproval in an amusing sketch with a message asking the drivers to leave space for pedestrians.

Georg Ratzinger, Joseph's brother who would later become a musician, once recalled an event that occurred in this square in 1931 when Cardinal Faulhaber came here to officiate at a confirmation.

Along with the other children, the young Joseph – Georg's junior by three years – welcomed the cardinal with joyful songs, but was so impressed by the blood red of the Archbishop of Munich and Freising's cassock that he shouted out: "One day I will be a cardinal, too!" Alarmed by this outburst, Georg immediately attempted to calm his brother's enthusiasm. "But only two weeks ago you wanted to be a painter," he said. Perhaps – and who knows? – this really was a sign which unexpectedly communicated itself to the heart and mind of the boy on that confirmation day when the Holy Spirit was present in abundance.

An alley now led us to a cobbled street. Here, the gardens were immaculately kept. It was the season for roses, and a number of varieties of them were in flower, each a different colour. Walking past La Sicilia, an Italian pizzeria, and leaving the church of St Lawrence on our right, we arrived at the nursery school that the Pope had attended.

The shouts of children at play reached us from the windows of the first floor. We sat down on a low wall. Gloria looked at me and shared a reflection that had occurred to her. "In a world in which everything is changing continually, it is nice and also relaxing to see that here, things have progressed in the most simple and genuine way." I agreed.

In the year 2005 this nursery school celebrated its 120th anniversary; and in the same year Joseph Ratzinger became head of the Universal Church.

We now visited the church of Allerheiligen (All Saints), which, as the Pope has said, is a great favourite of the Ratzinger family. In 1983, as a cardinal, Joseph Ratzinger celebrated the 300th anniversary of its foundation. It was built by Bartolomäus van Opstal of Salzburg, and even today its ancient splendour is intact. Visitors can still admire the Baroque altar in black and gold, the precious rotating tabernacle that was built in 1760, and the statues of St Augustine and St Monica, witnesses to a past in which Augustinian friars lived here. I also noted the confessionals that still had their violet curtains, and the stucco pulpit in the Salzburg style.

We then walked up to the old fortress. Inside the courtyard, now excavated, we spent a moment enjoying the cool of the shade and the splashing of the fountain.

Looking around, I realised how successful Bavaria had been in preserving such places, where not even signs advertising restaurants are allowed. They have also managed to limit commercial and industrial development near the old town centres. Here there is none of the terrible speculative development that has blighted Italy and even our most ancient archaeological sites; and yet they have not lost out either in terms of industrialisation or of sustained development of the service sector.

We now followed a lane leading down from the fortress and through the woods to the Ponlachkirche. It was the same lane that Georg, Maria and Joseph walked along as children when their mother took them to this place of peace and prayer.

We sat down on a pew in the small church. The door behind us was open, and we could hear the babbling of the stream in the woods. Now that I was here myself, I began to appreciate why the Pope is so attached to his homeland. It is clear that these places had a profound effect on him from childhood onwards.

How does the character of a boy develop when he lives in a country town and walks through the woods with his mother and brother and sister to venerate the Madonna in a small votive chapel? The answer is obvious: the example set by parents and the family's way of life are essential factors if children are to

IN THE FOOTSTEPS OF JOSEPH RATZINGER

grow up healthy and well-balanced and if religious faith is to be transmitted.

The Ratzinger parents were very devout and taught their children to be pious. On Sundays, Joseph, the father, went to the first Mass at six in the morning, then to the one at nine, and also to the last one in the afternoon. At home, he and his wife recited the rosary, read from the Holy Scriptures, and instilled in their children a sense of the value of the liturgy.

What a contrast between this and the families and upbringing of modern children who are all too often dragged around from the cinema to McDonald's.

They were simple people, these parents. The father, a policeman, was rather strict, but upright and intelligent; and his job gave him an early appreciation of the true nature of Nazism as it tightened its grip on a troubled Germany that was struggling to recover from defeat in the First World War. Then there was the mother, a good and gentle woman, loving towards her children, and a wise and responsible educator.

Throughout his career as a priest and as an increasingly well-known theologian, the future Pope expressed the affection and gratitude he felt towards them, as well as towards his sister who, he was to recall, was always ready to help him and Georg. He also made considerable efforts to reconcile the demands of his calling with his desire to keep his family united and to look after his ageing parents.

The story is often told of the simple but at the time quite usual way that his parents met – through an announcement in a Catholic newspaper. The young policeman was looking for a girl who shared his faith and who knew how to 'cook and also sew a bit'; and with the healthy Catholic realism that has borne much fruit in the past, he would not be displeased if she had some money of her own.

Nowadays, on the other hand, it is the romantic model of

love and marriage that dominates, even among believers. This is all very well while the initial passion lasts. Christian love is far more demanding, but also more rich and rewarding. It was indeed Benedict XVI who encouraged a deeper understanding of this in his first encyclical, *Deus caritas est.*

On the way back we met a young man who greeted us with a broad smile. I asked him what he thought about the Holy Father, and he jumped at the opportunity to tell us how proud he was to have a Pope from his own country. "He's written some beautiful books," he added in perfect English, "and is carrying on along the same road as his predecessor. He's a farsighted man." As though in a flashback, I remembered the headline of the popular German newspaper *Bild* on the day that Benedict XVI was elected. *Wir sind Papst,* it announced: "We are Pope".

In Gloria's opinion, among the towns we visited, Tittmoning was the most fascinating.

Traunstein – the most beautiful town in the world

The next morning we left for Traunstein. Here, it took us some time to find the house in which the Ratzinger family lived from 1937 to 1951.

After a while, however, we saw a sign saying *Papst Benedickt XVI Weg*, pointing us along the route for Pope Benedict. We drove past small houses surrounded by old-fashioned wooden fencing until we finally reached an old farmhouse dating back to 1726 and built in the Alpine farmers' style (photo 35). Ratzinger was thinking of this house when he wrote the following words: "Having led an itinerant life for so long, it was here that we found our real home, which I always remember with gratitude."

We were now in open countryside which offered a complete contrast to the town of Tittmoning. Because of the mist, I could not see Mount Hochfelln and Mount Hochgern, both of which are so dear to Ratzinger, who calls them the 'domestic mountains'.

The trees in the garden were laden with fruit, and we were tempted to pick a few plums, but were promptly dissuaded by a sign saying 'no entry'. It seemed likely that since the young man who once lived here had become Pope, the visitors were not only more numerous but also more invasive.

We sat down on a bench by a track that led into the deep green woods nearby, and Gloria read out a few passages from the Pope's autobiography. We tried to imagine how we would have felt if we had lived there as young girls. The Ratzinger children must have had many an adventure in the old hay barn, the woods and the fields.

This countryside offers a taste of the rural Bavaria that has survived up to the present day. The painted farmers' houses are neat and well-kept, often with decorative designs on the outside, whilst a variety of flowers adorn the balconies.

Behind the farmhouses are stables for animals, wooden sheds for the machinery, and barns in which to store corn, maize and firewood.

Gloria explained that nowadays all this was mainly a sort of show subsidised by the government in order to create the image of an untouched rural Bavaria, and that without massive central funding, the production of various crops would never be economically viable.

She also pointed out that the machinery used for making milk and cheese was modern and sophisticated, and went on to question the level of funding aimed at preserving certain traditions.

I would prefer it if this were not the case. I much regret that without subsidies farming no longer allows those who work the land to earn a reasonable living. As a tourist who is not involved in local politics, I find this part of Bavaria full of sweetness and beauty; and perhaps this is partly thanks to the cultural influence of neighbouring Austria.

One and a half miles away, at 5 Rosenheim Straße in the town of Traunstein, is the building that once housed the grammar school to which the young Joseph walked every day. Nowadays it is a music school. With the improvement in public transport over the years, you can get there on a convenient train that whistles whenever it departs.

Before going to what Ratzinger describes as 'the most beautiful town in the world', we visited the small church of St Anna in Ettendorf. Every Easter Monday the mounted procession in honour of St George finishes here.

In the meantime, the mist had risen, and from this small hill overlooking the valley there was a clear view of the 'domestic mountains'. I also glimpsed the outlines of the bell-towers and churches of Traunstein.

I could imagine the happiness of the two Ratzinger brothers and of the mayor's son Rupert Berger when, radiating grace as newly-ordained priests on 8 July 1951, they made their way along these narrow country lanes. Having celebrated their first Mass in the church of St Oswald, they walked from village to village, accompanied by an orchestra. The emotions attendant on such an experience were simple yet strong, pure and deep – the source of unforgettable memories that the Pope recalls with these words: "It was most of all during processions and the blessing of houses that I appreciated the extent of people's need for priests."

It also occurs to me that the strength of his attachment to the country in which he grew up perhaps forms the basis for the huge breadth of vision, the generosity of spirit, and the profound tolerance inspired by charity, all of which are the hallmarks of this Pope.

Walking round the centre of Traunstein, I was perhaps slightly influenced by the fact that as a cardinal, Ratzinger had described this as "The most beautiful town in the world." Once again, I was struck by the attention to detail that was evident everywhere. A coloured plaster statue of the Madonna and Child was attached to the wall of a seventeenth-century house painted pink; and it was covered by a small onion-shaped dome above which stood a shining gold cross, in the style of Bavarian bell-towers.

In the middle of the Marktplatz there is a fine fountain with a statue of St Leonard, the patron saint of farm animals; whilst nearby, two large mosaics of King Maximilian of Bavaria and St Benedict are incorporated into the yellow façade of a seventeenth-century building.

It is a well-known fact that the expansion of the Benedictine Order in Bavaria encouraged the spread of Christianity in the rest of Europe; which is why St Benedict is venerated so extensively here. To this very day, the motto *Ora et labora* ('Prayer and work') is widely recognised as an ideal rule, though one which is not always respected.

Today more than ever before, for somewhere to be considered attractive, it must first be safe, clean and silent; and according to these canons, Traunstein is a splendid place.

There was also the usual museum in honour of the homeland. In the bar just a few paces away from the doors of the church of St Oswald, Italian was spoken.

We now went into this church in which the Ratzinger brothers offered their first Mass (photo 34). Joseph celebrated it at six o'clock in the morning in a ceremony shorn of all non-essentials; whereas the Mass which Georg celebrated was accompanied by music. The interior of the church is in High Baroque style, with massive piers along the nave; it is full of frescos and decorative plasterwork, and even the old wooden pews have survived the forces of secularisation.

As in most Baroque churches in Bavaria, the nave is flanked by small side-altars honouring local patron saints and also the Virgin Mary. St Oswald, to whom the church is dedicated, looks down from a painting that shows him distributing his wealth among the poor. Born around 600 AD, this saint was the son of a pagan king and was baptised by Scottish and Irish monks.

We left the church and headed for the main square, a charming place in the shape of an amphitheatre and surrounded, as usual, by houses with brightly painted façades. At the end of the square was a large *Maibaum* – the may tree whose history goes back to popular pagan culture.

I went into a shop specialising in folk music and in which a large selection of musical instruments was on sale, including harmonicas. As we will see, the young Joseph Ratzinger was given one of these by his father when the family lived in Aschau am Inn, and he developed a passion for the instrument.

Among the many other retailers was a tailor-shop selling traditional costumes, near a branch of Antalya, the Turkish restaurant chain. Of the foreign communities in Germany, the Turkish one is the largest, numbering about four million; so that nowadays you will find not just Bavarian fare at an *Oktoberfest*, but also numerous doner kebab stalls.

We sat down in a restaurant with a view over the square, and I ordered *Weißwürste* and fresh *Brezen*. I confess that I was becoming very fond of Bavarian food, with its great variety of sausages, soups and desserts. There was however just one problem: after a few days my mouth was full of ulcers and my cholesterol level went sky-high.

Gloria is an amusing travelling companion, and a great entertainer. Perhaps this has something to do with her desire to defuse the fact that she is always almost recognised; with the result that in order to avoid coming across as the haughty princess, she lets no opportunity pass to have a laugh with people. So here, in this restaurant, she regaled the waitress with the following funny story: "Before putting the bill down on the table, the owner of the restaurant politely asked his clients if they had eaten well. The answer was not very enthusiastic: 'Yes, it was good,' they said. 'But we've had better.' So the restaurant owner replied sharply: 'Not here!' "

At the Seminary of St Michael

After the usual photo session that the proprietress of the restaurant insisted on having with Gloria, we went to the Seminary of St Michael to meet its new director Fr Mark Moderegger – an efficient-looking young priest, most attentive to the needs of his pupils; wearing a grey suit, a light blue shirt, a burgundy tie, and a small gold cross in his button-hole.

It was in this college that Joseph Ratzinger joined his older brother to pursue his studies at grammar school level; and the school reports of our Pope were unanimously favourable, except for physical education, which he himself has described as a 'torture'.

During the Second World War the college was turned into a hospital. Together with the other members of his class, the young Ratzinger was first sent elsewhere to continue his studies as best he could, and was then drafted into an anti-aircraft battery near Munich.

From the Pope's own writings, we know how the chaos of Germany's defeat meant that he had to move from Austria, where he had been sent to a work camp, to American POW camps at Bad Aibling and Ulm. From here he would return home only in the spring of 1945. Of this Calvary he was later to comment as follows: "The months after the reconquest of liberty, which only then we learned to truly appreciate, are among the happiest memories of my life."

Although the Chiemgau-Gymnasium is still called a seminary, it is really a college that provides a Christian education. Ever since it was founded, about ten percent of its pupils have entered the priesthood.

The large school buildings were built by Cardinal Faulhaber in 1929.

We went up some old flights of wooden stairs with a metal balustrade. Hung prominently on the first floor is a large portrait of the founder, and beside this is the photograph of Benedict XVI with his arms raised to the sky on the day of his election. "When the news came that a former pupil had become Pope, there was much celebrating among the students," said Fr Moderegger.

On the second floor we went into the chapel where the Ratzinger brothers celebrated Mass every morning when they returned to Traunstein as guests of the seminary. Above the altar is a fine painting of the Deposition of Christ, framed by two columns of blue enamel with gilded ivy leaves. The white cassock worn by Joseph Ratzinger is still hanging in the sacristy.

On the large desk in the apartment that was made available to him stands a vase in which there is always a freshly cut rose.

As a cardinal, Ratzinger was a regular visitor over the years, and was always accompanied by his brother Georg. The two of them liked to spend the period following Christmas here. Their last visit was in January 2005.

There is, I think, an attractive message for young people in the fact that the Pope has always been faithful to his own background and roots. Rupert Berger, the other seminarian who was ordained into the priesthood at the same time as the Ratzinger brothers, has also remained a good friend. He later became a distinguished professor of liturgy, a subject about which he has published a number of volumes, and he still lives in Traunstein.

Fr Moderegger also told us about the daily routine of the Ratzinger brothers when they came here for a break. First, holy Mass, then breakfast, then the newspapers, then a walk, during which they were always seen talking animatedly. Then came administrative work, followed by lunch with the nuns.

After lunch, it was off to the music room, where Joseph played the piano and Georg the organ; and the day's activities concluded with another walk before it got dark. Before leaving on the last day, they would always walk into the town, however cold and wet it might be, to buy small thank you presents for the nuns and the director of the school.

I must say that the more I hear such details, the more I am filled with admiration. They are solid people, these Ratzingers, well tempered for life and its difficulties, but also open to friendship and able to sustain it over long periods not only with people, but also with places; their lives are full not only of prayer and serious study, but also of music, of healthy walks, and of sociable meals; these are balanced existences, with no sudden breaks or ruptures, and in which a productive present serenely recalls and relives the past, while also looking to the future. Their faith seems to have produced people who are truly fulfilled, capable of showing great creativity and also deep and mature love.

As we were leaving Traunstein, I could not fail to recall a story that Georg Ratzinger told me about how after the Second World War, the Salzburg Festival no longer attracted such a large international audience as before, with the result that the cost of tickets and of hotel rooms became affordable. So he got onto his bike, and on this admittedly not very rapid means of transport travelled to Salzburg to buy tickets. At the time, a hotel room with breakfast included cost three marks. So the two brothers had various opportunities to listen to their beloved music, including Beethoven's Ninth Symphony conducted by Hans Knappertsbusch, and Mozart's Mass in C Minor. . . .

To the Monastery of Au and to Aschau am Inn

We now set off to visit the scene of an earlier period in the Pope's life – the Monastery of Au, where the young Joseph took harmonica lessons and his sister Maria was educated.

From the road we saw a continuous succession of whitewashed houses with balconies and flowerboxes full of colourful primulas; whilst crucifixes and small shrines were dotted here and there in the fields (photos 23 and 24).

All this brought to mind some words that the Holy Father spoke about his native country and which now took on an even clearer meaning: "We remain anchored in our own Bavarian spirit because it is a cultural identity. Our experiences during childhood and youth influence and inform the lives of each one of us. These are the true riches which we draw on for the rest of our lives."

Further on, we passed the spectacular medieval castle of Haag. We then stopped for a refreshing ice-cream at Da Esmeralda, the Italian *gelateria* on the main road.

The journey continued through a succession of valleys, hills and woods (photo 22). No sooner had we passed the Peterskirche (photo 37) than in the distance we spotted the much photographed Monastery of Au am Inn (photo 36).

Nowadays this former Benedictine monastery, which later passed into the hands of the Augustinian Order is inhabited by twenty-two Franciscan nuns. In the charming *Biergarten* nearby, customers were merrily quaffing jugs of beer.

We went inside the seventeenth-century church. I was stunned by this show of so much splendour; this was perhaps the most beautiful place we had visited so far.

In the picture of the Assumption above the altar, the Virgin Mary wears an expression of joy that is almost contagious. The fresco in the cupola above is full of angels and cherubs playing instruments and singing songs to celebrate the arrival in Heaven of the Mother of God. It felt as though we could almost touch the hilly countryside that surrounded the monastery outside the large church windows. The ancient pews are real masterpieces of carved woodwork.

The side-altars, of which there are about fifteen, are all sumptuously adorned with hand-made lace altar cloths; and the one dedicated to the Pietà – the Virgin Mary holding the dead Christ – is surely the most moving, with every detail perfectly conceived for the worship of God.

I cannot help thinking that some of our Italian parish priests should come here in order to appreciate how important it is to love the house of the Lord. It is precisely this love, also expressed in small things, which ensures that the Mysteries of the Faith are less removed from the People of God. Formal worship is of course the essential thing; but the beauty of the building, the taste and harmony with which it is decorated, the music that accompanies the services – all these are most important. Like music, beauty brings us closer to God and opens the road to Him. The reason for this is that when the soul is elevated, it is distanced from all that is negative and is encouraged to acquire the intuition which helps us to glimpse that supernatural element which, as is said, goes beyond but never conflicts with the natural.

We continued on our journey, and a few miles further on found ourselves in Aschau am Inn. Yes, once more we were on the banks of the river Inn, which is such a constant presence in the life of Joseph Ratzinger.

It was not so much farmers, but the employees of large metal factories who lived here.

We went inside the church of the Ascension, where the future Pope made his first communion.

It is so fresh in my mind that I cannot help recalling the meeting that took place in St Peter's Square, one Saturday afternoon on a mild October day in Rome, between Benedict XVI and a group of children who had come from all over Italy to make their first communion. With his usual kindness and simplicity, the Pope shared his memories in the silence of the crowds that filled the square: "It was a beautiful Sunday morning in March 1936. The sun was shining, and music was playing. There were about thirty boys and girls from my town. The essential thing about this memory is that I realised that Jesus had come into my heart. This was a gift of love, and one that was full of joy. I understood that a new stage was beginning in my life, and that it was important to remain faithful to this meeting, to this communion. And so I carried on with my life, thanks to God. The Lord has always lent me a hand and guided me, even in difficult situations. The day of my first communion was the beginning of a shared journey, and I hope that for you too, this will be the beginning of a lifelong friendship with Jesus, because it is in his company that life becomes worthwhile." Which of us might say the same?

The house in which the Ratzinger family lived from December 1932 to the spring of 1937 no longer exists. On the main road that runs through the village, the place where it once stood is marked by a stone plaque bearing the papal coat of arms and is now a place of pilgrimage. Two Polish priests stopped there and made the sign of the cross, after which they took photographs of each other. They wished to preserve the memory of this moment, I thought, and also of this place which is a memorial in its own right . . . a memorial to a boy who, even then and as he himself later wrote, sensed the presence of the Mystery, and for whom the Lord had great designs.

As we have seen, the Ratzinger family had to move from one place to another many times and within the space of a few years, before settling down for good in Traunstein. Some of these moves were due to the work of their father, a policeman for whom this was part of the job; whereas others were dictated by a desire to flee from the growing pressures of the Nazi regime which were felt particularly strongly by Ratzinger's father, opposed as he was to what he saw happening around him.

It cannot of course have been easy for the children to reintegrate themselves each time, and to change habits, schools and friends; but in the face of this, the family remained united in faith and love. As soon as Maria, the older sister, left school, she went to work and helped pay for the education of her two brothers; whilst Georg and Joseph continued with their parallel lives, supporting each other as they went.

Our tour of the scenes of the childhood and youth of the future Pope was at an end. The next day we were due to return to Regensburg.

VI

REGENSBURG – A SMALL ROME

A town on the banks of the Danube

The countryside around Regensburg is very different from that in the area where the Pope was born. The hills are less gentle and rolling, and we are now in the extensive European forests referred to as 'the green roof of Europe'.

The German name Regensburg – I prefer the Latin name Ratisbona, which sounds less harsh – comes from the river Regen, a tributary of the Danube which takes its own name from the ancient Roman military camp, Castra Regina.

The Danube, the great river which flows across the heart of Europe to the Black Sea, has served as Regensburg's 'main road' ever since this navigable waterway formed the natural northern boundary of the Roman Empire.

Not only does it carry boats laden with merchandise, but it also dominates much of the life of the inhabitants of this charming Bavarian town. The embankments serve as promenades for enjoyable walks, whilst along the natural banks there are numerous places where one can sit down for a beer and a taste of the local specialities.

I much enjoy walking or bicycling along the charming medieval streets in which you can still see the remains of various Roman towers and gates, of which the locals are very proud.

Then there is the famous bridge, the Steinerne Brücke, which is a real masterpiece of medieval engineering. Built in 1135 entirely out of stone, for many centuries it provided the only crossing over the river.

If the old centre of Regensburg is a world, then this bridge is a world within a world; always busy, and on fine days home to street artists and musicians, and much else besides. If you walk along its full 302 metres, you will soon be met by the unmistakable smell of the sausages frying on the grills of one of the largest and best-known local eateries which welcomes you as soon as you reach the other side of the river.

If Rome has more than one thousand churches, the far smaller Regensburg has fully three hundred.

The most beautiful of these, in my opinion, is the Alte Kapelle, which is near the cathedral, in the very heart of the old centre. I find it enchanting and almost moving, with its sumptuous abundance of extravagant and colourful high Baroque decorations (photo 39).

In one of the side-chapels there is a famous Byzantine icon showing the Virgin Mary. It is remarkably similar to another image of the Madonna known as *Salus Populi Romani*, which I love very much and which is in the Borghese Chapel in the basilica of Santa Maria Maggiore in Rome. The icon here in Regensburg was given to the Holy Roman Emperor Henry II by another Pope whose name also happened to be Benedict – although this time it was Benedict VIII.

The citizens of this ancient imperial town have a different mentality from the inhabitants of Munich. The *Regensburger* are friendly but distant; they are very proud of their history and think of their town as a stronghold guarding various wonders.

It is also an unusual place in that the citizens have not let the houses in the old centre be taken over by offices and institutions, as has happened so frequently elsewhere. Partly as a result of this, the atmosphere here is happy and lively. When the weather permits, the inhabitants pour out onto the streets and crowd around the tables of the bars and restaurants in the numerous squares. In this love for life in the open air, they are like the Romans.

Until the 1960s the Protestant community was larger than the Catholic one; but the last thirty years have seen a marked reversal of this situation.

The cathedral of St Peter has for centuries been the very heart of the Catholic community here. Ever since the Middle Ages, its famous children's choir – the Regensburger Domspatzen – has sung every Sunday and on major feast days, without once breaking this great tradition.

Since his brother Georg has been *Kapelmeister* here for thirty years, Benedict XVI has an almost fraternal link with this most famous of choirs which performs worldwide.

Over the years I too have attended marvellous services here, thanks to which I have come to appreciate the extent to which music and singing are not just an embellishment of the act of worship, but an integral part of the Mass. In the words of Benedict XVI: "Solemn sacred music that includes choir, organ, orchestra and a singing congregation is not an addition that makes the liturgy agreeable; it is, on the other hand, an important means of active participation in the act of worship."

A popular religious festival

Gloria and I were now invited by the bishop to attend the inauguration of the cathedral's west door, which is in fact its main entrance. The ceremony was a most enjoyable spectacle, and not just from the aesthetic point of view. All the young choristers were there in their best red cassocks and white lace surplices, lined up in front of the cathedral waiting for the arrival of the bishop – Gerhard Ludwig Müller, a man richly endowed with spiritual gifts and numbered among Germany's great theologians;

this being a further reason for the friendship, respect and affinity that exist between him and the Holy Father.

For years, one part or another of this immense cathedral had been undergoing repairs. But for the previous few days no trace of scaffolding had hidden its glorious Gothic architecture from view. This was certainly due to the imminent arrival of the Pope.

I was witnessing a genuine popular religious festival. Here, the brother of His Holiness is known as *Meister*. Everyone likes and respects him. However, on this important occasion, he hid behind the other priests, since he has always been extremely modest, shying away from all forms of unnecessary publicity.

The procession made its way past members of the congregation who were surprised to see the Blessed Sacrament leaving the cathedral to be deposited in the nearby church for the all-night adoration. I realised that even here, young people no longer knew how to behave in a profoundly spiritual situation; and so, feeling out of their depth, they did what came naturally, grabbing their mobile phones and raising them high to take photographs.

Here, I reflected, was one of the problems of our times – the youth of today have no knowledge of traditions. Often this is the fault of parents who, in order to feel free themselves, have not respected these traditions, most especially where religion is concerned; and very often their children have simply imitated them.

Looking around, I was impressed to see the town decked out with flags bearing the papal coat of arms. Never could I have imagined, during my previous visits to Regensburg, that I would one day return to Gloria's town to await the arrival of a former German cardinal who was now Pope.

The Pope's cooks and a bishop from Kenya

That evening we stayed in the town and ate at the Bischofshof restaurant near the cathedral. For many years the cook here,

Herbert Schmalhofer, had been in domestic service with the von Thurn und Taxis family; then he and his wife Monika rented premises from the bishop and set up a restaurant which is now considered one of the best in the town.

It was the Schmalhofers who catered for the Pope and his entourage during his stay in Regensburg. Even when they both lived in this town, or when the future Pope used to return here on long breaks from Rome, the Ratzinger brothers used to go to Bischofshof, mainly to eat a dessert washed down with lemonade or – and I am told this was on rare occasions only – by a sweet wine.

The cardinal's favourite has always been the *Kaiserschmarrn*, or 'the Kaiser's mishmash' – a pancake made with almonds, raisins and sugar, and which is cut up into pieces while it is being fried.

We sat down, and a few minutes later were joined by Frau Agnes Heindl, a dear friend of Gloria's, and by Martin Kivuva Musonde, a young bishop from Kenya.

Since she became a widow, Agnes has been housekeeper to Georg Ratzinger, and in this capacity has been an important and valuable presence for the Pope's brother, who is now elderly and has serious problems with his sight. One would never guess that this lively lady was more than eighty years old; her eyes are always smiling, and her heart is always ready to attend to the needs of the *Meister*.

This charming octogenarian invariably wears a hat and has a weakness for shoes with at least a bit of a heel. Her brother Hubert Schöner is also a priest, and in his capacity as chaplain and deacon of the Alte Kapelle, he had the honour of receiving the Holy Father when he came to Regensburg to attend the inauguration of the newly restored organ.

Agnes and Hubert have been devoted friends of the Ratzinger brothers for years.

I enquired after the reason for the presence here of the bishop from Kenya, and was fascinated by the story that I heard and that enabled me better to understand the heart and mind of this sweet-tempered lady who was a guest at our table.

Twenty years before, a young seminarian from Mombasa had spent a period in her house, when her husband was still alive. Having returned to Kenya, the young priest invited her there to attend his first Mass. Agnes was very recently widowed, and her daughter saw this invitation as a good way of preventing her mother from dwelling on her recent loss.

And so mother and daughter set out for Kenya. The deprivation and poverty that they saw there affected them profoundly, and Agnes decided to do something to help these people. With her own hands, and with the help of the young priest, she started to build a retirement home for priests and nuns.

Over the years this priest became her main contact in Mombasa and her right-hand man for this project. From that moment on, the intrepid Agnes went to Kenya every year to check progress; and apart from taking the funds that she had collected in Germany, she stuffed her suitcases with clothes for the missionary priests, and even with discarded church vestments that she had repaired herself. During the pontificate of John Paul II, this young priest was made Bishop of Machakos.

This man was once more the guest of his beloved German *Mama*, and was soon to meet the new Pope.

Bishop Martin Kivuva Musonde was now fifty years old, a cheerful man with the ready smile that the Africans so often have. He also has a strong character and is a gifted communicator.

I asked him what he thought about the important problem of celibacy for African priests. He confidently dismissed the question, insisting that it had been conjured up by the mass media. He also said that from his own direct experience and knowledge gained from numerous African priests, celibacy is for the most part not their main concern!

Agnes and her bishop had just returned from a pilgrimage to Lourdes. For the young African bishop, this had been his first visit to the Pyrenean shrine. He had been profoundly affected by the way in which people had searched for God in that sacred place.

Meister Georg

I had already met Georg Ratzinger, His Holiness' older brother, at Passau in October 2005.

There is a clear physical resemblance between the two brothers, and they have a similar manner. Whilst one wins you over with the subtle intelligence of the great theologian, the other does so with the sensitivity of the musician; but they both succeed in reaching the hearts of others.

Georg is charming, friendly, and full of humour. Shy and rather retiring, he has found himself the object of intense media scrutiny ever since that fateful 19 April 2005, when his telephone started to ring non-stop, while hoards of journalists camped outside his house at Luzengasse.

He is a simple and spontaneous man. Once, at an event in which I was also taking part, someone pointed out that his clerical jacket was buttoned up wrong. He allowed it to be put right for him, admitting, with a wicked smile, that he did not always cut the smartest of figures.

Today I had been given the job of collecting him from his house and taking him to have lunch with Gloria (photo 41) and a few other mutual friends. When I rang the bell he asked me, over the intercom, to come in and wait a moment in his sitting room, since he was running slightly late.

It was a welcoming room, full of religious objects and with a large photograph of his brother the Pope. A picture of him playing the piano also hung on one of the walls, and I immediately recognised this as the work of Dina Bellotti, a great Roman portraitist who had unfortunately died a few years previously, and who had been a friend of the then cardinal and a frequent guest at his house in Rome. I too had known her well and had loved her for her value as a person and for her sensitivity.

When the *Meister* appeared, he thanked me for having come to pick him up and asked me, with a humorous glint in his eye, what he should call me. "Just Alessandra," I replied. Timidly and almost doubtfully, he repeated the name. "Alessandra, Alessandra. . . ."

We talked about Rome and various mutual friends, then made our way towards the front door. The *Meister* held on tight to the white stick that he uses because of his impaired sight.

He refused to be helped, and like a gentleman, stood aside to let me go first. As was now often the case, a small group of onlookers were standing outside the house, which was decked out with yellow and white ribbons and papal flags. He did not seem particularly put out, greeted them politely, and sat down in the back of the taxi.

On this same day, Benedict XVI was flying towards his native country which awaited him, expectant and curious. Georg had not rushed to the airport, where he would be in the limelight, but was to see his brother two days later in Altötting.

In Gloria's house, where other guests were waiting for us, we sat down to eat almost immediately.

Inevitably, the first toast was drunk to the Pope who was returning home to visit the places and people in which and among whom he had been educated and had grown up; important places, as we have seen, and ones to which he has remained deeply attached and to which he had frequently returned during his years as a cardinal in Rome.

Georg knew well, however, that this was no sentimental journey that his brother was making. Joseph Ratzinger is first and foremost the Vicar of Christ, and his first priority is always his universal mission.

Necessarily, the relationship between the two brothers changed when he was elected to the papal throne. Thus whilst as Pope, Joseph Ratzinger took on all the responsibilities of his position, Georg preferred to stay in Regensburg, his home town, protected by lifelong friends and content to go to Rome two or three times a year.

Trips out of town and holidays spent together in the places they had known as children were now distant memories; as were the times of relaxation when Joseph played pieces by Schütz, Bach, Vivaldi and Monteverdi on the piano for Georg, who in his turn played other pieces that they both loved. Gone, too, were the large meals in the cardinal's house in Pentling – always ready-made food, since neither of them knew how to cook; and as for the ritual of washing up the dishes, that too was now a memory.

As lunch proceeded, the conversation moved on.

Talking about his father, Georg told us that he had been strict but fair, whilst his mother had been especially sweet-natured. "She immediately understood that what both sons wanted was to go to the seminary, and she never tried to prevent us in any way."

The conversation was interspersed with highly amusing stories, since the *Meister* is an extrovert who likes to play to the gallery.

However, he has the same kindness, serenity, modesty and calmness as his younger brother. He likes talking about his childhood, but does not like questions that are too direct. "We were entirely free to decide for ourselves," he said. "I wanted to become a priest, and since I was three years older than my brother, I was the first to make my choice. Then Joseph followed in my footsteps."

Those who know him well sense a certain regret for the fact that he has, inevitably, lost a degree of intimacy with his brother. It is now almost impossible for him to spend time alone with his beloved Joseph. On the other hand, as a priest he views the Pope with all the love and respect felt by a man of faith who appreciates the value and responsibility of the mission that now weighs on his brother's shoulders.

Regensburg – home to the family

For the last forty years Regensburg has been home to the Ratzinger family. The two brothers also took the remains of their parents and of their sister Maria there. The bodies of their mother and father, who had died and had been buried in Traunstein, were exhumed in 1974 and transferred to the cemetery at Pentling, a suburb of Regensburg.

In February 1964, shortly after the death of his mother in 1963 (his father had died several years before), Georg was appointed *Kapelmeister* of the cathedral and director of the Domspatzen, its famous youth choir.

"Having until then been at the margins of our lives, Regensburg now became a focal point for us," wrote the then cardinal in his memoirs. "It was there that we met in the holidays and there that we felt increasingly at home."

Indeed, after his years as a professor at Münster and Tübingen, which had involved no small degree of controversy and theological discord, Joseph Ratzinger was offered – and accepted – the chair of Theology and Dogma at Regensburg University. The opportunity to bring his family together was certainly a major factor in his decision to build a small house on the outskirts of the town, near his brother, and where he could live with his sister Maria. These were happy and important years, during which the three Ratzingers renewed old bonds.

This situation continued uninterruptedly until, one day, the radio announced the sudden death of the Archbishop of Munich. Some time afterwards, Joseph Ratzinger received a visit from the papal nuncio who handed him a letter from the Pope appointing him to the vacant post.

Later came the years in Rome, as Prefect of the Congregation for the Doctrine of the Faith, during which period the then cardinal returned whenever he could to Regensburg and to the other places in Bavaria that were dear to him.

A discreet visit to the Pope's house in Pentling

Cardinal Ratzinger had hoped that once freed from his obligations in Rome, he would be able to retire for good to the small two-storeyed 1950s-style house set in its garden on the leafy outskirts of Regensburg (photo 42), here to pursue his theological studies in peace.

The last time he had spent a carefree period had been in January 2005, just a few months before being elected Pope. In the sitting room, a small wall calendar with pages that you tear off for each day, is witness to this. The date is frozen at Friday 7 January (photo 43).

Before the Holy Father arrived in Bavaria I asked Gloria if she could possibly arrange for me to look around this charming residence and also round the cemetery where Ratzinger's parents are buried along with his sister Maria.

This wish of mine was certainly not inspired by any streak of voyeurism, which, I believe, is something that I have never had. However, I have always been interested in the way the last two Popes from abroad – the Polish John Paul II and the Bavarian Benedict XVI – have lived their lives. Perhaps because of their temperaments, or perhaps because they grew up in environments that were different from those of the Italian Popes who preceded them, the fact is that they have both brought something new in terms of personal style.

Although orphaned at a young age, and in spite of the fact that a bloody war was in progress, John Paul II faced this difficult situation with courage, labouring hard in a quarry and in a factory, whilst at the same time feeding his lively and profound soul with poetry, acting and sport. He was able to relate to people with different mentalities and faiths and to build deep friendships with them; and having become first a priest and then a bishop, he preserved a style that was serious and engaged, but also at ease and receptive towards everything good and fine that life offers and which the Incarnation, whose witness he is, caused him to appreciate. Thus even as Pope, he continued to write poetry and somehow find the time to swim and ski, to go for walks in the mountains, and to commune with nature.

Benedict XVI, on the other hand, received the God-given gift of growing up in a family rich in faith and love, and in a nucleus that protected and aided him for many years, without ever preventing him from becoming a man who was solid and serene, and receptive to beauty and friendship; a perceptive and profound theologian whose considerable qualities soon gave him prominence, who desired to use his ability as a thinker to bring and explain the Christian faith to the people of today, whilst remaining balanced and careful not to compromise the Truth itself, nor to see it obscured under a mass of hazardous and often dangerous intellectual hypotheses; a man of great intelligence, but simple in the details of his everyday life, and with a profound and well-ordered spirit, but never cut off from events around him.

Two men of God therefore; and not only two Popes, but two priests with deep faith and great talents, but by no means 'clerical' in their approach. And I say 'clerical' on purpose, referring to an approach that distances the sacred from the mundane and encloses it in a sort of fenced-off area; an approach that might suggest that God is not present in everyday life or in a daily existence that is simple, but also lived knowingly and deeply, with love for everything that is beautiful and good, wherever these things manifest themselves.

That is why I now wished to visit this small house in which the future Pope spent his days here in Bavaria, together with his brother and sister. I was sure that I would find this a moving and enriching experience.

Agnes Heindl found the time to act as our guide on this rather special visit.

We started our tour at the cemetery of Ziegetzdorf in Pentling at whose entrance there is a large black crucifix with Christ's body in shining gold. Small gravelled paths lead from one tomb to another. Everything is neat and extremely clean and well-kept.

At the back of the cemetery, near the hedge that surrounds it, is the grey tombstone on which are carved the names of the Ratzingers' parents and of their sister – Joseph and Maria, and Maria again. It would be impossible to find a more Catholic set of names.

Two ladies from Regensburg, both friends of Agnes', change the flowers to ensure that they are always fresh and sweet-smelling.

The Pope's house is a few hundred metres away, and is immediately recognisable because it is the only one in Bergstraße to have a brand new wooden fence. This was a present from the students of the vocational training college in Amberg.

A few tourists were posing for photographs.

A coloured plaque on the front of the house announces that this is the residence of Benedict XVI, and for those wishing for further information, it even gives the telephone number of Rupert and Terese Hofbauer, who have looked after the house and garden since 1977, when Ratzinger moved first to Munich, and then to Rome.

On the ground floor, there is the kitchen where the Ratzinger brothers enjoyed preparing their ready-made meals, and also a sitting room that looks out over the garden. Agnes Heindl told us that *Meister* Georg wants to make this the house's chapel. A large wooden crucifix was already on the wall, and two church candlesticks stood on the floor; but there was no *prie-dieu*.

Gloria and I exchanged looks, and announced, almost in unison, that we could see to getting one.

No sooner said than done. Gloria rang the man who looks after the furniture in the Schloss St Emmeram and asked him if he would be kind enough to bring her best *prie-dieu* (photo 45). So now the room in the house in Pentling that has become a chapel contains the *prie-dieu* which for many years was in Gloria's bedroom in the Schloss St Emmeram, and on which she knelt every evening to pray in front of the small image of the Our Lady of Good Counsel of Gennazzano.

Through the french windows I spotted three bee-hives in a corner of the garden. "My little paradise," was how the cardinal was fond of describing this green space around his house. The small amount of honey that is produced here is still sent to Rome by Herr and Frau Hofbauer. I was moved by the simplicity of this small detail, and thought of the man who was first cardinal and now Pope receiving, from time to time, various specialities from his native land – pastries, honey, *Weißwürste* and perhaps other things that we did not find out about. . . .

We went upstairs to the first floor. Here, there is a small square table at which, we were told, the cardinal used to write. A teddy bear sits on a comfortable *chaise longue*, bringing to mind St Corbinian's bear. A 1950s sofa and armchair and also a low table with numerous objects on it and various still-unopened presents stand against the wall; and there is a small bookshelf to one side.

Out of respect, I did not go into the bedrooms; but the door to the bedroom of the Ratzingers' sister Maria was ajar, and from outside I glimpsed a table with a number of rosaries on it. I thought about this good and simple woman who, when her brothers were preparing for the priesthood, had always been willing to help out, not only with her own earnings, but also by typing for them.

Unlike Georg and Joseph, she did nothing remarkable that will go down in history; but she is remembered for an evangelical humility that made her almost invisible. I am sure that not just the memory of his mother, but also the memory of this kind and simple woman have contributed to the understanding of the female world and its richness which is such a hallmark of Benedict XVI.

Terese Hofbauer came up to us to say hello, carrying a large and fine-looking cat in her arms. This was Chico (photo 44), who was friends with the Pope. "The cat often used to follow the cardinal around when he was walking in his garden," she told us. This neighbouring couple, who look after Benedict XVI's house, know they own a treasure – never has there been so much interest in a feline!

Chico is a seven-year-old tabby cat with brown stripes on a pale gold coat; by nature he is solitary and independent, and does not like to be picked up and stroked. He reminded me of Romeo – do you remember? – in Walt Disney's *The Aristocats*.

Before returning home we stopped to pray briefly in the church of St Joseph in Pentling, where the then cardinal often helped the parish priest.

The Pope's arrival in Bavaria

The days had gone by and our journey in the footsteps of Joseph Ratzinger was now over. There remained the final chapter – the arrival of the Pope himself in this, his native land of Bavaria.

We were going to try and be present at some of his public appearances in various places; but mainly, we intended to follow his progress – and perhaps even meet him – in Regensburg, where he was due to stay the longest.

The theme of this apostolic journey was "Those who believe are never alone" – a phrase close to the heart of Joseph Ratzinger, and which became the title of a song that was composed in honour of the Holy Father and was sung in all the churches in Bavaria.

Nor was this song the only nice surprise. When, at the beginning of the last century, the weather here was sunny, which was not very often, it was popularly referred to as *KaiserWetter*, or the Emperor's weather. This was a reference to the Habsburg Emperor Franz Joseph and to what appeared to be a strange power of his; namely, that it never rained during military parades and great public gatherings.

Today, the Bavarians have coined another term: *PapstWetter*, or the Pope's weather. Indeed, Benedict XVI's apostolic visit – and perhaps Providence had a hand in it – was marked by a series of glorious sunny days which made this historic stay in his homeland even more special.

It is well-known how in the heart of his homeland, the Pope repeated his evangelical message several times, with its central theme of the rediscovery of God and of faith.

In homilies and in meetings during those days, he addressed numerous issues, stimulating reflection and also reactions. Once again, his style was sober and lucid; and as always, one of his objectives was to explain that belief is not something complex and boring. Indeed, Benedict XVI never tires of repeating that there is one God, that He is Love, and that He chose to meet with us in the person of Jesus.

Because Christianity, the Pope repeated, is neither a philosophy nor an ideology, but an encounter with a Person who can radically change our lives. This is the message that he also explained so magisterially in his first encyclical, *Deus caritas est*.

A few hours before the *lectio magistralis* at the University of Regensburg, I was lucky enough to experience the joy of taking part in the open-air holy Mass on Islinger Feld. I was sitting next to Professor Alf Zimmer, the rector of the university, who told me with what great interest and excitement the other professors were awaiting the visit of their former colleague Joseph Ratzinger, unanimously considered one of the great thinkers of our times.

I believe that the address that the Pope delivered at the university a few hours later lived up to their expectations, even though we all know what happened subsequently: the inaccuracies and deliberate distortions in the press – mainly, I am afraid to say, in the Italian press, which is always looking for the next scoop; the violent and in many cases uncontrolled reactions from certain sections of the Islamic world; but also the calm, considered, but firm reaction of the Pope.

It is my opinion that what we witnessed after the address at the University of Regensburg was not just a direct attack on the Pope but also a defeat for freedom of expression. The storm in the media resulting from the misinterpretation of a medieval text quoted by the Pope unleashed reactions that were quite disproportionate. We were obliged to listen to the Islamic camp condemning the Holy Father to death and threatening to destroy Rome. This in spite of the fact that Benedict XVI had humbly explained that he had no wish to offend any other religion.

It was an ugly episode, and one that prompted the reflection that in our free and democratic world we will increasingly have to learn to use language that is not only politically correct, but also Islamically correct!

Leaving aside subsequent reactions to the address in Regensburg, Benedict XVI's time in Bavaria was one of great joy and was also a considerable personal success for the Pope himself, adding to his standing not only in Bavaria but also in Germany as a whole.

In this country which presents a number of challenges for the Catholic faith, though theology has for a long time been studied even in state universities, it seems that people have started to see this Pope as a man of dialogue, as a calm and intelligent figure. And perhaps precisely as a result of this visit and the direct contact that it brought, those who presume to oppose Benedict

XVI on a theological level will find life a bit harder than before. He is, after all, a German who speaks the same language, and whom most people in his country see as 'one of them'.

Friends together in St Emmeram

In St Emmeram, the huge complex that embraces the palace of the Thurn and Taxis family, there was also joy and excitement. The house was full of friends and family from all over Europe. How could they fail to be present for Joseph Ratzinger's visit to Regensburg?

To call the Schloss St Emmeram 'a house' might provoke a few smiles. But with at least five hundred rooms, it is indeed one of the largest private residences in the world, comparable to Buckingham Palace. I have seen numerous palaces, private and otherwise, around the world, and I have to say that few are so beautifully kept. I admit that every time I enter the courtyard, I feel moved and also respectful, thinking of the people who have managed to ensure that a tradition lives on whilst being adapted to the needs of today.

Gloria lives in a wing of the castle in which there is a perfect harmony between ancient and modern, with many modern works of art on the walls.

A young Belgian couple, guests of Albert, asked if they could look round the palace and the old monastery. I never say no to the chance of seeing something special, even though I already knew this place. So I took advantage of the opportunity and joined the small group for a glorious stroll through the reception rooms.

Every room is decorated in a different colour; and the one with the silver ceiling is certainly the most interesting. Walking through the throne room in which the prince elector used to receive the court during the imperial diets, we reached the spectacular ball room lined with armchairs upholstered in red velvet with embroidered borders. There must have been at least two hundred of them! The walls were hung with splendid Gobelin tapestries and with nineteenth-century paintings in the Romantic style.

A side-door led from the palace to the twelfth-century cloister of the Benedictine monastery, again named after St Emmeram, and thought to be one of the oldest in Bavaria. In 1812, as a result of the process of secularisation, it became the property of the von Thurn und Taxis family.

The crypt of St Wolfgang lies below the late Baroque church, whilst relics of the saint are preserved in a nineteenth-century casket under the high altar.

We returned to the palace and carried on discussing the events of the previous days: the fascinating figure of the Pope, and also the impact of his message, which had given renewed strength to the faithful and also seemed to have breached the defences of luke-warm believers and of non-believers.

Regardless of their social position, all people, in the depths of their hearts, face the same problems. They might not all perhaps have financial worries, and although that is no small thing, it can be precisely this material wealth that distances them still further from the Truth, so that they often end up not being tempered by the difficulties of real life and therefore living in a separate world, thinking that what they possess is enough to save them.

But that is not the case; not by a long way. No-one saves himself by his own efforts alone! Material abundance, great fortunes, even a cultured mind and a knowledge of science and the arts – none of these things, by itself, enables us to reach that goal. Only the intuitive knowledge that we are creatures forming part of a divine plan, and only a living encounter with Him who loved us first, granting us the gift of existence and then watching over us step by step – only this can give real sense to our lives and impart true joy to life. And often all this is sensed most quickly and fully by those whom their circumstances have made more humble or who have contended at an early stage with difficulty and suffering.

That very evening I had confirmation of all this.

Before returning to my bedroom for the night I was stopped on the stairs by Doris, a thirty-year-old black lady full of energy and curiosity. She looks after Gloria's house in Africa and had been invited to spend the summer in Germany as a reward for her excellent work.

She too had entered into the spirit of these special days, and her enthusiasm for what she had seen encouraged her to come straight to the point. "I want to become a Catholic," she said, looking at me with her large dark eyes wide-open.

Her statement came as a surprise, since during my stays over the years in Gloria's house in Africa, I had noticed the lack of interest there in our Church. Furthermore, the parish priest in Watamu in Kenya had always told me how unlikely it was that anyone belonging to an evangelical sect should convert to Catholicism.

Very gently and attentively, I asked her to try to explain the reasons for this change of heart of hers. "I have realised that your faith is based on love and kindness towards our neighbours," she told me, "and I feel a great need for this love."

I was struck by such simplicity, and also by such intuition. As the Apostle St Matthew says, the most simple people are sometimes truly the wisest. Doris had indeed understood the heart of the Christian message!

I gave her a fraternal hug and asked her to think it over a bit more before taking any hurried decisions, since I did not want her conversion to be a short-lived flame. I promised to pray for guidance before advising her how to start her journey down this new road.

Doris closed the door and departed, leaving me alone in the

silence of my room. Kneeling down, I tried to make myself small, including in the physical sense, and I huddled in on myself. I thanked God for having allowed me once more to see His love at work, so alive and so near.

A surprise audience, and a great and unexpected treat

The Pope's visit to Bavaria and Regensburg was drawing to a close. Since his schedule was so full, we did not know whether we would be able to meet him. But on the last evening, we received a surprise: the gatekeeper at the palace informed us that the police had arrived to take us to the seminary, there to meet the Holy Father.

We all rejoiced, and in an atmosphere of general euphoria, we got into the minibus. Pilar was also with us: the daughter of Gloria's sister, this attractive girl is unfortunately handicapped. Max Georg, a dear friend of the Thurn und Taxis family, was at the steering-wheel and ready to leave, but the police seemed to be in no hurry. Two policemen then got out of their car to inform us that the Pope was running late because his house in Pentling, which he was visiting, was surrounded by the faithful, and he was greeting each one of them individually.

Police headquarters had given orders that we were not to leave before the Pope reached the seminary. We tried to explain to the policemen that anyone attending a papal audience is expected to be there before the Pope arrives, and not the other way round. But there was nothing to be done. No offence meant, since every nation has its good and bad points; but flexibility is not a quality that the German people have.

Gloria was beginning to worry. Her son Albert, however, went back into the house and returned with a tray laden with drinks for anyone who might want them. In the meantime, while we were becoming increasingly agitated, the two policeman who were to escort us as outriders on their motorbikes took off their helmets and started taking photographs of each other in front of the old fountain in the courtyard of the palace (photo 40). Notwithstanding the importance of the audience to which we were going, I could not refrain from laughing, since even though I was in Germany, I felt as though I were in a scene from a film by Alberto Sordi. I reflected that throughout the world, things are very much the same.

The minutes ticked by and nothing seemed to be happening; so we decided to recite a rosary to calm ourselves down and to entrust our fate to the Virgin Mary. At least another hour passed before the order arrived for us to set off.

Just as we finally reached the seminary, and after so long spent waiting, Pilar shouted out that she needed to go the lavatory urgently. We had little time to spare, but the matter could not be put off. I offered to accompany the girl so that Gloria could go ahead, but she wanted to attend to Pilar, to whom she was both aunt and godmother.

Meanwhile Gloria's mother, together with her sister-in-law Clotilde Liechtenstein and the young Amelie, were taken to the first floor and shown into the room where the Holy Father was. I looked around, hoping that Gloria, Albert and Pilar would reappear. But there was no sign of them. I tried to stay calm and accept this small *contretemps* with good grace as one of the limitations that are part of all human things, even the nicest.

In one hand I was holding the small gilded wooden angel that Albert had taken from its position above his bed in order to give it to the Pope, and I handed it to a policeman. I just had time to put a scarf on my head, and before I knew what, I was standing before Benedict XVI.

I knelt down, kissed his ring, and then broke the ice. "Your Holiness, for a moment I feared that the Bavarians were not going to let you leave again, after such a successful visit. But you are going back to Rome tomorrow, aren't you. I hope we have nothing to worry about." The Holy Father laughed heartily and, with his usual kindness, replied that I need not worry, since his fellow-countrymen would certainly allow him to leave.

Having greeted his brother Georg and his secretary Mgr Gänswein, both of whom were present at the audience, I explained to the Holy Father why Gloria was late. He replied amiably that he was aware of the problems faced by the carers of the handicapped and of the attention that the latter needed.

Then, with the greatest kindness, he invited us to sit down, and we did so on small seats arranged simply around himself and his brother. I took this opportunity to make a further compliment. "Your brother is the best possible advertisement for the Catholic Church," I said. The Pope was pleased, as he always is when his brother is praised.

I was much struck by the fact that even though he had just returned from a walk-about in the crowds, he was relaxed and made us feel very much at ease. He told us that he had met and greeted a large number of people in every place on his itinerary.

He next asked us if we had been present, that morning, at the ceremony in the Alte Kappelle, that masterpiece of Baroque church architecture. I confessed that we had followed him around more or less everywhere; including, obviously, for the inauguration that same day of the newly-restored organ. "Your brother once explained to me," I said, "how new influences made themselves felt on sacred music in the nineteenth century, and how Gregorian chant and the polyphonic classical tradition were combined as part of the process of liturgical development. But your address this morning made it even clearer to me why in every little church not just in Bavaria, but throughout Germany, there is an organ in good repair and an organist too. You explained so clearly that 'the organ is king of musical instruments because it takes all the sounds of Creation and resounds with the fullness of human emotions.' "

The Pope smiled, and so did his brother. With this talk of music, the atmosphere in the room seemed to become more relaxed and harmonious. I admit that I have a healthy jealousy of this musical tradition which is still so alive, whilst ours in Italy no longer exists.

I have noticed how the Ratzinger brothers like to compare social realities and customs to the rules of music, and I well remember how Georg Ratzinger, speaking of the new pacemaker that he had to have fitted urgently during the Pope's first summer at Castel Gandolfo, dismissed his heart problems with the following words: "Like in a concerto, there have been a few discords in my heart, but now all is resolved."

That same morning in Regensburg, the Pope had said that "just as on the organ the expert hand must always and repeatedly bring disharmony back to harmony, thus we too in the Church must, with the help of divine gifts and grace and through communion in the faith, always find harmony in the worship of God and in brotherly love."

The conversation flowed freely for a few more minutes, after which the others finally arrived. The Holy Father immediately rose to his feet to welcome Pilar in her wheelchair. He made the sign of the cross on her forehead, and then greeted Gloria and Albert (photo 47).

We all sat down again. Returning to the discussion about the organ, Clotilde Liechtenstein said that in the church that morning, on hearing the first notes of Bach she had sensed the glorious triumph of the Church. Kindly as always, the Pope pointed out that "the Church has had her moments of triumph, even though it would be best not to use this word today, since there are in fact many problems to be solved."

He then turned to Albert and asked him when he was due to return to his university in Scotland. "It must already be cold there," he commented with concern. He also asked after Gloria's daughters, who were unfortunately not present since they had had to stay in England.

Albert then asked the Pope how he had spent his day off-duty. After a conspiratorial glance in the direction of his brother, the Holy Father gave his answer. "We went to the cemetery to pray at the tomb of our dear ones. Then we went to my house and cooked a meal as we always used to, although we were not allowed to wash up. We prayed together and meditated for a while. After that, Georg and I had an excellent lunch at his house in Luzengasse, a place which you all know well." To which Gloria's riposte was: "Excellent and abundant, I imagine!"

The audience was at an end, the Pope took part in a photograph (photo 46) and then said goodbye to each of us in turn, giving everyone a rosary.

Outside the seminary we met the bishop, Gerhard Ludwig Müller, whom we greeted with much joy and enthusiasm before returning home. In the car, silence reigned. We were all reliving, in slow motion, the precious moments that we had spent together.

Bavarian by adoption

The next morning, we were all sitting round the breakfast table with enormous smiles on our faces, discussing what we had felt during the audience with the Pope in the seminary. Each story had its own nuances and its own tenderness.

I turned on the television. The Bavarian channel was showing the papal helicopter leaving Regensburg. The camera followed it until it was over Freising. These were Benedict XVI's last hours in his beloved native land.

I too was due to return to Rome that afternoon. I could not hold back my emotion, and two tears rolled down my cheeks. A few minutes before, Gloria and the others had been joking about how, fearless as ever, I always managed to make the Pope smile with one of my light-hearted comments. But now I was overwhelmed by what I felt welling up inside me. I could feel the great joy that I had received during these days of pilgrimage flowing through my veins and right to the centre of my heart.

The memories raced through my mind; these days would always be unforgettable. Perhaps the most beautiful journey of my life had just come to an end.

Never had I felt such a strong link with this land of Bavaria, to which, in the end, I owe my return to the faith. There could be no doubt: my conversion, which started by Lake Starnberg in those now far-off August days, made me feel Bavarian by adoption.

EPILOGUE

From Regensburg to Istanbul

At first sight, this brief epilogue or postscript might seem to have little to do with the rest of this book.

But as I wrote the last of these pages, I was also covering Benedict XVI's visit to Turkey, which took place between 28 November and 1 December 2006. I had the good fortune to be in the Pope's entourage and to experience this important event directly. It was a historic journey during which the Holy Father once again showed himself to be the best possible shepherd for our Church in these difficult times.

It was also a challenging visit, full of snares and potential dangers; a journey which, more than any others, put the Pope to the test in the most arduous fashion. His mission consisted not only in visiting and giving heart to the tiny Catholic community in Turkey and in meeting his Orthodox brothers, but also in laying to rest the dispute that had raged ever since his visit to Bavaria, as a result of his much publicised address in Regensburg. That is the first good reason for returning, in this closing chapter, to a theme that links this university town in Bavaria to the city of Istanbul.

The second reason has to do with the subject matter of this book, and even more with the character of Benedict XVI himself and those human, intellectual and spiritual gifts of his – partly the fruit of his experiences in Bavaria – on which I hope to have shed light in the present volume by visiting the places where the Pope was born and grew up and where he matured as a man and as a priest; it has to do with the gentle but at the same time strong character which I perceived by meeting friends who had known him better, and which was so much in evidence during his visit to Turkey.

Worried by the protests from Islamic fundamentalists, numerous people in the Catholic world had advised the Holy Father against this visit.

However, the atmosphere surrounding John Paul II's visit to Turkey in 1979 had also been tense. At that time, too, massive security measures were taken, so much so that the Pope was sometimes transported by helicopter. Furthermore, Ali Agca, now serving a life sentence in prison, had declared in the pages of the Turkish daily newspaper *Millyet* that he would kill the Pope. "I will kill the commander of the crusades who arrives in the guise of a religious leader," he had announced. And as we all remember, Agca did indeed carry out his threat two years later, on 13 May 1981 in St Peter's Square in Rome. In other words, any apostolic visit had met and would always meet with resistance from a certain radical type of Islam.

But strong in the consciousness of his roots, Joseph Ratzinger, the Pope from Bavaria, had no intention of abandoning this journey. Having departed from Rome without fanfare, he managed, with his humility and sweetness, to win over the Turkish people, hour by hour. In four extremely intense days which I will always remember, events took an unexpected turn and actions proved more powerful than words.

The demonstrations and the dummies dressed in white and burned in the middle of the streets – things which were shown for weeks on the television – are now a matter of history. As a witness and close observer of events, I can state that the success of this visit lay in the personal achievements of Joseph Ratzinger. In the space of a few days he outlined the possibility of pursuing a common path, despite differences of culture and religious faith.

The most important moments of this visit, and ones which will long remain in our memories, were the meeting with the Turkish prime minister Tayyip Erdogan, the fraternal embrace with the Ecumenical Patriarch Bartholomew I, and the moment of prayer in the Blue Mosque with the Mufti of Istanbul.

Benedict XVI wished to visit Turkey because together with Palestine, it is considered part of the historic sacred of the Church. This is where the roots of early Christianity are still to be found; the Apostles and St Paul were active in Antioch, in Tarsus, and in other towns in Anatolia; whereas Ephesus was the home of St John and the Virgin Mary, and Mary's house (Meryem Ana Evi) is a shrine that is still much visited, even by Muslims.

I was struck by the fact that the Pope's first visit to a Muslim country (out of 72 million inhabitants only 32,000 are Catholic) took place in the very land in which Abraham (whom Judaism, Christianity and Islam share as their patriarch) undertook his journey of faith in God; setting out from Haran, a village in what is now Turkey.

But let us move on to the Pope's arrival in Turkey and to his long-awaited meeting with the prime minister. During the flight to Ankara, we journalists had not been the only ones to worry about this. For days, Tayyip Erdogan had expressed indifference towards the Holy Father's visit. "I don't plan my diary around the Pope's diary" had been just one of his many tactless statements. Looking back with the detachment that time brings, I think that it was the Pope's humble and diplomatic acceptance of a public snub that brought round the Turkish prime minister, who broke with protocol and welcomed Benedict XVI as he stepped off his aeroplane; and of course it was also a shrewd political move aimed at making a good impression on the western world, whose eyes were turned towards his country.

There has been much talk about the fact that Joseph Ratzinger changed his mind about Turkey's entry into the European Union, and that during this visit he commented appreciatively on the effort the country had made to prepare itself for the negotiating stage. But the historic opinion of a cardinal, as Ratzinger then was, cannot be set against the evaluation on the part of the man who had now become Pope.

Turkey asked to be admitted to the European Union in 1987, and in 1999 was given the status of 'candidate country'. After years of preliminary dealings, negotiations started in October 2005 and will last at least another ten years. There are not a few issues on the table: human rights; the recognition of Cyprus; the management of the Islamic fundamentalism which exploded after 9/11 and is increasingly invading the secular Turkish state; and finally, the thorny question of religious freedom and the legal recognition of non-Muslim minorities.

Benedict XVI was the third Pope to visit Turkey, although the list should perhaps include Angelo Roncalli, Blessed John XXIII, who was apostolic delegate to the country for ten years. Paul VI visited Istanbul, Ephesus and Smyrna in 1967; and this journey saw his historic meeting with Patriarch Athenagoras I, which marked a new stage in ecumenical dialogue and the rapprochement between the Catholic Church and the Orthodox Church.

There have been special links of fraternity between Rome and Constantinople over the centuries. For the first thousand years the two sister churches flowered together, whereas for the thousand years that followed the links were weakened by distance. The Great Schism took place in 1054, when Leo IX and the Patriarch Michael I Cerularius excommunicated each other. In 1979, when he met Dimetrios I, John Paul II said that he was in Istanbul "to express a firm desire to continue along the road that leads to full unity between all Christians."

Ecumenism has always been close to the heart of Benedict XVI too, as he declared at the beginning of his pontificate. He also made it clear that he saw his meeting with Bartholomew I on St Andrew's Day as the main reason for his journey.

Joseph Ratzinger's visit also caused the Turkish press to turn their attention to the Fanar, the Vatican of the Orthodox Church; indeed, the Turks have never much liked the Patriarch, refusing to recognise his ecumenical status. In spite of that, and even though the Greek Orthodox faithful number only 2,500 in Turkey, among the leaders of the Orthodox churches he is still recognised as being *primus inter pares*, or first among equals, and is thus the leader of about 250 million faithful all over the world.

Following on from the dialogue started by their predecessors, the joint declaration by Benedict XVI and Bartholomew I restated their "heartfelt desire for full unity". The two religious leaders agreed to numerous practical things that they would do together, but the most powerful sentence in the document was certainly the one in which they announced that "to kill in the name of God is an offence towards Him." It was in effect a reiteration of what Ratzinger had said at the *lectio* in Regensburg.

The part of the declaration that dealt with safeguarding God's Creation came as a surprise for everyone, and was certainly inserted at the initiative of Bartholomew I, who for twenty years had been saying that one of the Patriarchate's priorities was the preservation of the environment; thus earning his nickname 'the green patriarch'.

In December 2005, again in Istanbul, I had had occasion to meet the so-called 'Pope of the East' in a close and informal way. He is a charming man, and also speaks perfect Italian, having studied at the Gregorian University in Rome. I remember how he told me that "peace is linked to the saving of our planet," adding that "the way in which we treat each other mirrors the way in which we treat our planet."

Faced with the devastating and atrocious images of today's wars, I have often thought about that observation. But knowing the open-mindedness and farsightedness of Benedict XVI, I am sure that during his time with Bartholomew he also thought about Moscow, the 'Third Rome', which conquered the sceptre of Orthodoxy after the fall of Constantinople in 1453. Perhaps, too, Alexy II observed the events taking place in Constantinople with pleasure.

After successful encounters with his Orthodox brothers, the Pope faced the far more difficult test of visiting the Blue Mosque, the most magnificent place of Islamic worship in the world, and one which has six minarets, making it second only to Mecca with its own seven. This visit had been suggested by the Turkish government only a few days before the Pope's departure from Rome, and was an unexpected invitation that he could hardly refuse.

What might initially have been seen as an act of provocation however turned into a providential opportunity for dialogue between cultures and civilisations. During the visit, the Mufti of Istanbul unexpectedly suggested to the Holy Father that they should pray together. Joseph Ratzinger was not the man to refuse such an invitation, and the extended moment of joint prayer was filmed by the TV cameras.

Within a few minutes these images had been beamed round the world; representing, as they did, an important gesture of friendship and respect between the two religions. My immediate thoughts were not about this, but were ones of great emotion, since I saw this as a clear demonstration of the Pope's thinking. As he had explained to us the day before, "an authentic dialogue between Christians and Muslims must be based on truth and inspired by a sincere desire to know each other better, respecting differences and recognising what there is in common."

These were profound and emotive reflections. It occurs to me that this great Bavarian Pope is now passing on to us Catholics throughout the world the gifts that he has received in the course of his life: true and serene love from his family and his friends; a grounding in a profound and sincere faith; the culture of a land that is full of life and the joy of life; and a fundamental soundness of character that enables him to be a truly free instrument of the Holy Spirit. Thus Joseph Ratzinger, a man who is profoundly faithful to his roots and to his identity as a son of Bavaria; a man who, coming from a rural background and from small provincial towns, was formed and tempered as a priest by his years lived fully and intelligently as a Christian – for precisely these reasons, as Pope he is truly open to the world and to its various cultures.

This clear identity of his, rooted in a religion to which he has borne witness every day of his life, makes him a man without fear. "From a spiritual and pastoral point of view, these were unforgettable days," he said on his return to Rome, where he preserved in his heart the memory of the small but exceptionally strong Catholic community that he had met in the very places where the Apostles had been at home. This was therefore an important journey for various reasons, not least because it renewed our hope, which is sometimes sorely tested in the face of wars, hatred and blind vengeance. With humility and gentleness, the Pope showed us how to live in peace and with mutual respect.